Naked Out Loud

Machan Taylor

NEW HAVEN PUBLISHING

Published 2025
First Edition
www.newhavenpublishingltd.com
newhavenpublishing@gmail.com

All Rights Reserved
The rights of Machan Taylor as the author of this work, have been asserted in accordance with the Copyrights, Designs and Patents Act 1988.
No part of this book may be re-printed or reproduced or utilized in any form or by any electronic, mechanical or other means, now unknown or hereafter invented, including photocopying, and recording, or in any information storage or retrieval system, without the written permission of the
Author and Publisher.

Cover Design (C) Pete Cunliffe

Copyright © 2025 Machan Taylor
All rights reserved
ISBN: 978-1-915975-28-7

In this stunning memoir, Machan Taylor traces her journey from postwar Japan to the world stage with Pink Floyd and Sting. Uprooted from an idyllic childhood in Yokohama, Taylor was thrust into a New Jersey suburb where she didn't speak the language and felt utterly alone. And yet she learned to turn devastation into song. **Naked Out Loud** is a meditation on identity, perseverance, and the courage it takes to come to terms with —and reveal—one's true self.
–*Patrick LaBella, psychoanalyst and painter, New York City*

This professional singer's story of the origins and path of her very successful career is especially compelling in the context of her bi-racial / bi-ethnic background, which made her feel she didn't belong, and seemed to dictate that she remain silent. Until, finally, she couldn't!
–*Margaret Daisley, Blue Horizon Books*

Sting, David Gilmour, Pat Benatar, Miles Davis and many others have recognized Machan's gift, and **Naked Out Loud** tells the compelling story behind it with candor and grace.
–*Mike Errico, Music, Lyrics, and Life: A Field Guide for the Advancing   Songwriter*

Machan speaks right to you, weaving the deep as the sea benefits she gained from her discoveries with psychedelics into her rich life story. She bravely invites you to ride along with her and take a look. Refreshingly real.
   –*Donna Sorgen LMHC, LPC psychedelic assisted therapist, teacher at Fluence, Woodstock Therapy Center, Woodstock, NY*

For my Grandmother Chie, my parents, my siblings, the seven generations before me, and the seven generations in the future.

May my offering of truth and love be healing.

I don't regret difficulties I experienced; I think they helped me to become the person I am today. I feel the way a warrior must feel after years of training; they don't remember the details of everything they learned, but they know how to strike when the time is right."

PAULO COELHO, from The Zahir (Caravan Publishing, 2005)

Content

Preface	8
Swimming with a Whale	12
To the Land of the Setting Sun	17
Suburbia and The Sounds of Silence	24
Stranger in a Strange Land	28
My Musical DNA	31
Music: My North Star	37
From the Music Box to Julep Joints	44
All Aboard!	52
The Jackson Victory Tour	58
I Wanna Know What Love Is	63
Seven the Hard Way Tour - Pat Benatar	69
Moody's Mood - George Benson	74
The Delicate Sound of Thunder Tour	79
Learning To Fly-The Delicate Sound of Thunder Tour	86
A Momentary Lapse in Reason	91
On the Turning Away	96
Roots and Realizations – Hiroshima	104
The Flip Side of Miles	110
What You Won't Do For Love - Bobby Caldwell	114
Panic at the Deposition	119
Exodus East	123

Back in the Big Apple	128
Out of the Blue	132
Childless Mother	138
Running Wild	142
Y2K and the First Sting	146
The Second Sting: Beginning the End	151
The Sting Operation	156
After the Rain Has Fallen	161
The Birth of a New Dream	164
The Day Everything Changed	168
Out of the Rubble	173
Country Roads and Ramblings	176
Ch, Ch, Ch, Changes	180
Time Waits for No One	185
Going Forward	191
Ramble On… Sing My Song	195
Acknowledgements	199
About the Author	201

Preface

"I can do nothing for you but work on myself. You can do nothing for me but work on yourself" - Ram Dass

It's said in certain circles that you're only as sick as your secrets. In American culture, we hide behind our status, whether it's our career success, monetary riches, or social media popularity. We use our outward presentation to protect our inner world and tender underbelly.

In Japanese culture, "saving face" (mentsu wo tamotsu) is a central concept that refers to maintaining one's reputation, one's standing in society, and one's personal dignity. Losing face is associated with losing the respect of yourself and others, resulting in a sense of failure and shame.

Because I was born a multi-racial person with Eastern and Western influences in my purview of life, it's been at times confusing as to where I belonged and how to be in the world. It's been a little bit of a purgatory, if you will. I had a very murky sense of identity as a child. Along with growing up in a very dysfunctional family system, I felt groundless and lost much of the time. I wasn't really white Anglo-Saxon, and wasn't really all Japanese. I wasn't really all Christian because my mother was at heart a Shinto Buddhist, believing in the laws of nature and reincarnation. My family was on the surface middle-class, but somehow always struggled. My existence felt like it was in the middle of everything and nowhere at the same time.

With all that, I somehow came into the world as a hungry seeker. As far back as I remember, I sensed that there was much more to life than met my eyes. I had a desire to know more. I always felt a profound depth and meaning to the world around me that I needed to explore and understand. Whatever was going on beneath the surface, in the belly of the beast, and veiled behind everyone's "face", was where my mind wanted to wander.

Now, at this later stage of life, I appreciate that I was born a sensitive person who has felt things deeply and questioned the why and how of the world around and within me. I can finally embrace this characteristic about myself and have found peace with it and who I am. That said, my sensitivity as a child wasn't easy to endure and made me feel awkward and out of place often. But that simmering discomfort guided me through nebulous moments and served as the fire pit of strength and a torch of faith that reassured me that all would be ok no matter what. One way or another.

I never imagined myself writing a book, and certainly not a memoir. I didn't think I was smart enough or interesting enough or that anyone would care enough to read it. But in recent years, I received encouragement from various people, and I began to think that I might have something of value to share, secrets to shed, and perhaps I could offer a little inspiration to others. I knew that doing so would require me to be vulnerable and expose parts of myself that have been hidden away in the shadows of privacy. And that it would require me to be willing to "lose face."

But rather than thinking of this book as me losing something, I decided to look at it as redefining an old concept. I found that the act of writing this book is a liberation from my mask, thus revealing my true face that's behind it. Perhaps the true meaning of losing one's face is an act of defiance and courage. It's the lifting of the veil, unlocking the proverbial chains, stripping off the burka, and burning the bra. It's denouncing a construct of behavior decided for me. It's making a statement of freedom derived from telling the truth. No longer hiding behind a manufactured sense of shame that society or someone else imposed upon me. I finally realized I don't have to accept the traditional or cultural meaning of the term "losing face". I can create my own meaning.

At this point in my life, I genuinely understand the saying, "hindsight is twenty-twenty." That idea can only make sense with a perspective woven from time and age. You can't stand two inches away from a Picasso painting and understand the intention of the entire work. It's only with distance and overview that you can take it all in. Such is the power and beauty of age. When we're young and building a life, it's impossible to have that advantageous perspective. We have so much time ahead of us and are entrenched in the process of living.

Now, as I experience time blazing by like a stream of bullets, I feel the call to resolve troubling issues, smooth out rough edges, and start tidying up some loose ends. Or, at the very least, make peace with my demons in the dark and the monsters under my bed. Beyond that, I contemplate what of value I can leave behind to honor this beautiful gift of life.

I hope this book serves as a little impasto technique: a palette knife of thick, broad strokes presentation, exposing emotional texture and colors of the picture of my life… for whatever it's worth to whomever it's worth. That's the beauty of art to me. It's an offering from the creator to be freely experienced and interpreted by the audience. With that, a creation takes on a myriad of existences through the hearts and minds of those who take it in. It's a kind of magic. Art is magic.

We all have stories to tell, and I believe they're all fascinating and consequential. These stories testify to our commonalities and differences, our heartaches and triumphs, and the truth of our shared human experience. Stories are an anthem to the miracle of our being alive. They provide us with a precious link in the continuum of our existence so we don't feel so alone. Because the truth is, we are spirits alone together, mysteriously spinning through the emptiness of space on this ball of Earth through time just for a little while.

With all the current conversations about mental health, trauma, spirituality, and such, I share my story as a contribution to that collective conversation, hoping it enriches our collective consciousness and evolution. It's only through our humanity and community that change can happen.

The truth sets us free from the burden of secrets, lies, and shame. I know this to be true because these encumbrances are what I've worked on unraveling all my life. I've worked on shedding the weight of those wounds as far back as I can remember. Isn't that really why we're here in this physical form? To know thyself and grow?

So, here, with you as my witness, my fellow human traveler, I humbly strip down layers of my being, expose some tender spots, abandon fears, and surrender shame, while losing "face" for you to have and hold however you will. I hope this is my best career performance yet, as I sing my song to you, "Naked Out Loud"

Swimming with a Whale

"The sea is the symbol of the collective unconscious, because unfathomed depths lie concealed beneath its reflecting surface" - Carl Jung

I was floating weightless, surrounded by a viscous, dark blue haze. Ethereal. Boundless. Slowly, I realized I was swimming in the depths of a vast ocean. It was deep, down, and dark, with just a murky glow of light radiating from the surface above me. My long dark hair was bobbing around my head with the waves of the thick liquid shrouding my naked body. Although I was swimming underwater, I breathed easily, carrying a peaceful sense of calm and freedom in this mysterious space surrounding me. How curious.

As I looked to my left, this enormous, dark grey body was swimming beside me. I recognized it was a giant whale. Its massive eye acknowledged me, letting me know all was okay. We were traveling together through this incredible wilderness of the sea. Strangely, I wasn't afraid. In fact, I was at peace in a way I had never known. It seemed the whale was my guide, my teacher, and friend, and we had been swimming together for a millennium.

As I gently paddled my arms in breaststrokes, the whale effortlessly glided beside me with a ballerina's grace. Astonishing for such a massive body! We were suspended in space, existing without time, without a sense of place or purpose. But the water can do that... create a sense of transcendent timelessness. It relieves one of the burdens of gravity and frees us from the weight of this flesh body; this heavy mortal vessel.

It seemed like I was submerged underwater for a long time without having to come up for air. But again, I had no sense of the time. It was as if I had turned into a fish or a mermaid, and the sea was my home. I felt at home.

After languishing in that feeling of infinity in that beautiful blue dream, I remembered what I was actually doing and where I was. I had awakened in my subconscious mind, and I was trying to make sense of what my spirit guides were trying to tell me. I was there to learn something important. Something that my conscious mind had kept hidden away for years, so that it wouldn't cause me any more unbearable pain. It's not that I was completely ignorant about these hidden truths. But my subconscious buried them like an iceberg, and it was time to explore more than just the tip. It was time to dig deep below the surface, explore its structure and mass, look at the details, and crack open the hidden treasures buried in the depths of my psyche. It was time for healing. I was ready. At that moment, I knew that the medicine was opening the door to a deeper realm of myself.

As I was coming to grips with what was transpiring, I began to explain to my therapist what I was seeing, feeling, and experiencing in my journey. Visions of my grandmother appeared before me. I started thinking about being two or three years old, and being held in my grandmother's arms. I remembered how warm and loving that feeling was. I hadn't thought about that for most of my adult life. I flashed on a picture I had brought with me to the session, which was sitting on the coffee table next to me, where I was stretched out on a sofa.

As I swam and drifted through the deep waters of my mind, fragments of my life as a little girl in Japan flashed through me. I had a visceral sense of being small. Bursts of images exploded in my mind's eye like quick clips of an edited film. I saw my house in Tokyo, the exotic landscapes, extended family, and unfamiliar places and people. But somehow, always cutting back to the thought of my grandmother and that sense of love and belonging that I had then, and had long lost.

Suddenly, all this emotion came flooding in. Tears started to swell from my stomach to my eyes like a giant ocean wave. This deep ache of sadness came bubbling up from my core like a spiritual volcano arising from the center of my world. Tears burned past my temples like hot lava. It was an eruption, an awakening, a cracking of old, crusted earth. It was a psychic purge. A birth.

I opened my eyes and sat up to look at the pictures on the table. There sat the ghostly images of my grandmother, my parents, and me as a little girl in Japan. I didn't even know why I had brought these pictures with me. But now it was keenly evident. The medicine was showing me that the heartbreak of leaving Japan when I was four years old was still actively alive in me and bubbling at the root of my being. The torturous sadness I locked up in my heart all these years needed to be acknowledged and find the light. It needed to be released from where it was buried and trapped. It desired acceptance for what it was. It wanted to be validated and accounted for. It was my trauma talking. And it needed to have its voice heard and have a long overdue conversation with me.

Trauma is a presence not to be reckoned with or ignored. It has a piercing reality and a darkness as unstable as quicksand. The only way to soothe it is to hold it in the light with consciousness. It will not accept anything less. Or it will play tricks on you, wreak havoc like a petulant child, and try to be the operating system of your world, running in the background of your existence like the Wizard of Oz behind the curtain.

Though I tried my best over the years to deny its existence and pretend that it was just a memory, some little annoyance like a paper cut, my psyche was no longer having it. Like a woodpecker stabbing at the side of my cedar-shingled house, it was calling me to the pain, to the source of the matter. No matter how many times I shooed it away, it kept coming back, tap, tap, tapping on my door, pecking for attention and comfort. No matter how I tried to bury the past, it refused to be left behind. At least for now.

Honestly, it wasn't until this pivotal moment in a non-ordinary state of consciousness that I realized how deeply scarred I was. That childhood experience of being ripped away from my birthplace, from the loving arms of my grandmother and my original family, stripped away my early sense of identity and being. It tore away everything my small child self knew. It robbed me of the only language my tongue could shape at the time. And ripped away the piece of earth I stood on. The pain was blaring a pentatonic, woeful song. The wound was weeping. And it was as wide as the Pacific Ocean between Japan and the US. My subconscious dutifully preserved those salty, bitter memories like preserved lemons or scientific body parts in formaldehyde. It is there in that black hole of the subconscious that the power of transmutation exists. The power of turning water into wine and dirt into gold awaits, if you dare to travel to those depths.

That was my first psychedelic-assisted MDMA therapy session in 2020. Powerful and transformative, it went beyond what years of talk therapy had ever delivered. That said, perhaps the preceding years of work prepared me to be able to dive deep into that space of raw, gut-wrenching discomfort. I arrived familiar with the landscape of my psyche, and the language of the mind field, which helped in that setting. I was ready to do the work of communicating with those lost parts of myself. I was braced to face the pain and gather the psychic treasure presented to me.

Taking that step would help me make sense of the hows and whys of so many puzzling past experiences. It helped to answer persistent lingering questions I had about my lack of self-worth and sense of emptiness. Hidden under the surface of what were glamorous and fantastic times on the surface of my life, lived a lonely, scared little girl struggling to cope and survive, uncomfortable in her adult skin, and searching for love and understanding.

This transformative moment helped me connect loose dots and unravel the threads of meaning in my personal and professional life. It showed me the roots of my emotional struggles at times, why things unfolded the way they did in my life, and, more importantly, why I reacted to those experiences the way I did. It showed me the cracks in the porcelain that needed to be mended. It helped me sort out what I needed to work on to heal the wounds of yesterday so I could reclaim my present and prepare for my future.

Those long-stored away memories gushed from within me in my first psychedelic-assisted therapy session. It made so much sense that I found myself swimming with the whale. It was the medicine that led me back to the beginning, the scene of the crime, and the original sin. It brought me back to reclaim that little girl and that abandoned piece of myself on the other side of the Pacific ocean. A little girl who felt abandoned and was so scared. It was time to reclaim her and see what she had to teach me. It was time to integrate her back into the embrace of my heart, fill in the missing blanks, and help me to be whole. I realized, too, how much I was missing that little girl, and how much she was missing me.

    As Gabor Mate says, "Trauma is not the bad things that happened to you, but what happens inside you as a result of what happened to you."

Grandma and me in Japan

To the Land of the Setting Sun

"Some journeys take us far from home. Some adventures lead us to our destiny" - The Chronicles of Narnia: The Lion, the Witch, and the Wardrobe

We left on June 29, 1959 on the USNS Fred C. Ainsworth, and arrived in San Francisco, CA on July 11th, 1959. According to the ship's crew and passenger list I was able to dig up, my family was listed as "Aliens". How strange and repugnant a label it was to see. To think that because we were Japanese, and other than white Americans, we were seen akin to creatures from outer space. I had to sit with that for a moment.

We were leaving Japan because, now that the war was over, my father had decided to retire from active military duty. Being married and with a family to think about, he needed work. Not being fluent in Japanese limited his possibilities in Japan. Also, being a "gaijin," or an outsider in Japan, made it doubly difficult to find employment. So he secured a government job in New York, close to where he grew up in Paterson, NJ, and where he had some family. Little did my mother or my sister and I know what difficulties awaited us with my father, his drinking and emotional problems, and living in America. Now, back to being an alien.

For most of my life, I repressed the reality of my so-called exotic ethnic mix and how I physically presented in the world. I knew, of course, that I wasn't "white." But I wasn't completely yellow or brown either. So my identification drifted in between the worlds of East and West. Us and Them. Neither here nor there. Or this or that. A kind of limbo of existence. My personal purgatory.

That betwixt place of not belonging to a clearly defined dominant "white" group in American society is a strange standing. I imagine anyone who is a darker shade of pale, or an ethnic blend, has felt these unsettling feelings at times: aberrant, deviant, or the "other". But the peculiar thing is that America originally belonged to the Native Americans, who are much closer in color to so-called "brown" people. So who should really be feeling out of place? And let's not forget that so-called "white" people, and all the various shades in between, are biologically genetic mutations of Africans. Chew on that for a moment.

The idea that I didn't fit in was a constant, gnawing sensation inside me all my life. Like termites chewing on a house frame, the very structure of my security felt threatened. It was a continuous trickle-feed drip of disgrace. Like a disease waiting to bloom, I worked hard to hide the dark underbelly of my dis-ease. My mission was to prevent my malignancy from rearing its ugly little head. I labored to "save face" in good old Japanese fashion however I could. And I fiercely covered up my awkwardness, like some horrible case of teenage acne.

Music and performing later became my perfect cover and ally. I found my superpower, personified magic shield, a song and dance distraction method that allowed me to divert people's attention away from the hidden truth of how I felt about myself. I found the perfect façade to fake a sheath of glitter and happiness. I picked the exact profession that would allow me, in fact, demanded that I hide in plain sight. It's all about the lighting and makeup, and the "ta-da" factor as a performer. It was the foolproof setup, and I had the goods to pull it off. I packaged myself up to present an appearance of a beautiful life even though I was an "alien" after all.

After our ship docked in San Francisco, we boarded a train, traversing east across the expanse of the country to New York. I don't remember much about our journey across the Pacific Ocean or our travels across the United States. I was only four. I wish I were old enough then to remember more details about that trip because, to this day, I hate cruise ships and love trains. I love how you can sit back, relax, and watch the changing terrain whiz by. It's pure entertainment to marvel through the window at the little towns going by and wonder what life must be like for the people living there. There's something old-world and romantic about it.

I've often wondered what it must have felt like for my mother and my older sister, Miyuki. She was old enough to understand what was happening. To take that long, monumental journey so far away from Japan, leaving family and friends behind, knowing we wouldn't return. It must have been devastating. My mother was thirty-seven years old in 1960. A fully grown woman with a career and a lot of life history by then. My sister was thirteen. She was an innocent, blossoming teenager, not speaking much English, and just at the beginning of discovering her individuality. To have their lives dramatically deconstructed down to a name on a manifesto, and to be handed a blank slate of a future, surely and dramatically affected them. I can only pretend to imagine how frightened they must have felt. But in true Japanese fashion, they never spoke about it.

At that age, I wasn't really cognizant of what was happening to us. But as research in neuroscience and psychology proves, those beginning years of life before the age of five are the most impactful and important developmental moments for the brain, the psyche, and an individual's personality. It's the launch pad for the trajectory of our entire lives. Even the first few months of life directly influence a child's sense of self and place in the world. Beyond that, the early years can determine one's ability to survive in the world: how we feel about the world, our sense of safety and comfort, our level of inherent anxiety, serotonin and dopamine levels in the brain, the kinds of relationships we'll have, our ability to deal with difficulties, our self-esteem, cognitive function, how we learn, etc… The list goes on. This is why I believe some basic training and a license should be required for anyone who wants to bring children into the world. It's a mammoth responsibility. Not one to be taken lightly.

With my father's family and job on the East Coast, we disembarked off the train in New York City. His sister Mildred, brother Bill, and their families would be our first lily pad in this strange new pond. Unfortunately, my father's parents had died when he was young. Or so the story goes. So there were no grandparents on his side of the family to welcome us with open arms, like the ones I had left behind. No one and nothing could replace that. But at least there was a place to go, and people my father felt connected to. Theoretically.

From what little I remember, my father didn't get along very well with his sister Mildred. He told me years ago that when he was a teenager, his parents had died in a car accident. Whether or not that's true, I'll never know. That's when he went to live with his sister Mildred and her husband Henry. Apparently, they were very strict and physically abusive toward my father. It's the reason my father got into boxing during his teenage years. And the reason why at the age of seventeen, he lied to join the military to get away from them. The Army was his refuge out of a bad situation, as it can be for so many young men and women who have little hope for a future, or few opportunities in life.

My father's early life is sketchy at best. I found out he was married to a woman named Madeline Mirando in 1944, according to Ancestry.com. I understand they had a son named Tom, whom I learned about through my mother when I was a teenager. But none of us have ever met. Shortly after my father and his first wife married, my father went off to war. The rest is unknown history. I have no idea what happened to Madeline or their son. But it's clear that secrets like these are the hallmark of dysfunctional families. Sadly, my father's story is a depository of skeletons in a hidden closet, where they will likely remain for all eternity.

By August of 1960, my parents bought a house in a typical post-WWII suburban neighborhood in Wharton, New Jersey. It was there where we would settle into our little version of the American Dream. It was a modeling of the collective aspiration for every white middle-class family to have a house in suburbia, a nice car, and all the modern conveniences that life had to offer. It was a time of massive wealth development for the middle class, the importance of status, the burgeoning economy, the birthing of corporate dominance, and one of the most revolutionary times, socio-politically, ever in modern American history.

That said, it's possible that this moment in 2025, as I write this book, could be one of the most tumultuous times in American history. It is the post-pandemic era. It's the first time in history a sitting president is a convicted felon. There is war raging in

Ukraine and Gaza. Roe v Wade has been federally overturned. The American government and democracy are being dismantled and taken over by tech billionaires and corporations. And we are only a few months into this particular administration being in charge. This is not the America my father fought for, or brought our family from the other side of the world to live in. God only knows where this all leads. I can only hope there will be a happy ending for humanity. And on the right side of history.

Me and my sister Miyuki before leaving Japan

 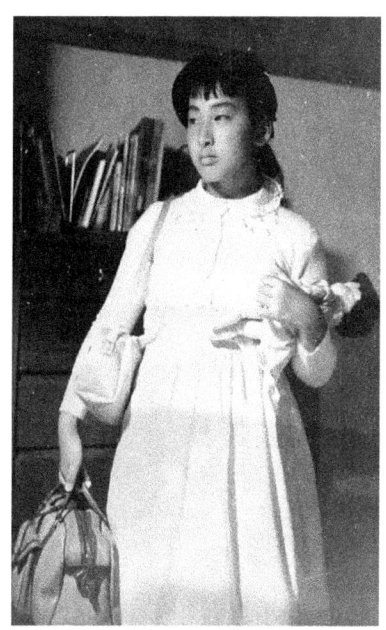

Saying goodbye to family at the port in Yokohama

The USNS Fred C. Ainsworth ship

From the ships' manifest

Suburbia and The Sounds of Silence

"Silence is the most powerful scream" – Anonymous

Settled into our New Jersey suburban life, my father took the train to New York City every day to work as a safety engineer. He worked for the federal agency OSHA in the Maritime Division. OSHA is the Occupational Safety and Health Administration, which oversees safety and welfare for workers. It was perfect for my father after being a Sgt Major in the Army and a police officer. He was good at giving orders and being an enforcer. The flip side of my father's personality was someone who could actually be quite funny and entertaining, particularly if he had been drinking.

In those days, when my father commuted between New York City and our little bedroom community town in New Jersey, bar cars were a standard amenity on the commuter trains. So my father regularly came home drunk at the end of his workday. Yet somehow, he routinely managed to do that commute for nearly thirty years. That said, there were many nights he never came home. That was the period when my father secretly had an apartment in NYC with a woman he was having an affair with. I don't know how long it lasted, but I remember my mother telling me when I was twelve or so about his philandering. There were many secrets and lies with my father that my mother silently suffered with. I think it's typical of a life with addicts.

Before that time period, when I was about eight or nine years old, my mother was forced out of being a stay-at-home mom to take a night shift factory job to help pay off my father's gambling debts. Mostly horse betting, I think. Our family was in financial trouble at one point, and on the brink of losing our home because of his out-of-control behavior. My mother worked for ten years assembling aerospace plastic components of some kind. Repetitive, mundane work, to help feed and clothe us kids. And more significantly, she labored to keep a roof over all our heads. It was a testament of my mother's love and dedication to our family for sure. I so appreciate and admire her for that. But it was also, in part, her being a martyr and an enabler for my father's brokenness. Because even with her sacrifices, he never changed.

It was around the time my mother started work that I remember being placed in the position of growing up and learning responsibility quickly. I had to learn how to cook, clean the house, help manage the property, and take care of my younger siblings, Jaqueline and John. My mother had to sleep during the day, so she needed a lot of help. My father was absent much of the time, and when he was around, he was usually recovering from his destructive behaviors. My older sister, being nine years older than me, was gone by the time I was nine. She left the house right out of high school and joined the Navy, where she met her husband, married by twenty-one, and went on with her life. Naturally, I was next in line to be the eldest child.

We never sat down to eat dinner together as a family, except on a rare occasion. We usually ate in the living room in front of the TV, which was constantly blaring. The din of the TV was the sonic backdrop of my childhood memories. It served as a salve to the thick, deafening silence that otherwise occupied the emotional tundra between us all. There was little honest communication that happened in our house. Of course, there was conversation about daily, superficial things, but hardly any words about inner feelings or genuine emotional connection. No instruction or guidance about life. No navigating difficulties or learning conflict resolution. We were related strangers sharing space.

Being a sensitive child, I remember feeling lonely and hungry for warmth and the connection that other kids around me seemed to have. We didn't take vacations or have family events. My parents didn't hug and say I love you. Some of that was most likely my mother's Japanese non-demonstrative nature. And the other half was my father's hardened, macho persona protecting his heart.

No surprise he drank and smoked so heavily and died of heart failure and the ravages of alcoholism. Also, I think emotional repression was just part of that generation's way of being. That was no fault of their own.

I remember the only honest expressions of emotion were my parents' screaming arguments. They mainly fought about money and financial struggles. I think too, that the angry dramas were a release. All those pressure-cooked, pent-up emotions that were pushing against the framework of the family had to go somewhere. Anger was a simple way to act out all the frustration, disappointment, and resentment that permeated the air. Though it was scary as a child to hear their arguments, it was also strangely satisfying. Part of me liked the drama, because it was a real sense of emotional expression, even though it was an incredibly damaging imprint. It was an unhealthy representation of adult relationships, which would later be reenacted with some of my own relationships, particularly with my first marriage.

Our house was generally a mess. My mother was a bit of a hoarder and became much more so later in life. As I understand more about that neurosis now, I see that material things became symbolic of holding on to a sense of safety and comfort for her. There were piles of papers, clothes, and other belongings taking up space all around the house. Remnants of her life in Japan and of the past. Materials that reflected her desires and dreams. She never threw anything out, which could also have been a Depression-era mentality. It's sad to think she felt so unsafe and unfulfilled. Regardless, it felt suffocating to me, though the house was basically kept clean. Consequently, I hated to bring anyone over to our house when I was young, because I was ashamed. To this day, I'm uncomfortable with a cluttered, messy home.

It wasn't until much later in life that I realized that I became an A-type personality, a caretaker, and a fixer, because of the role I had to assume during my formative years. Though it gave me skills and a sense that I could do almost anything, because I had to, it's not the way children should learn how to be adults.

According to the brilliant work of John Bradshaw, who is a prominent figure in the field of recovery and family systems, it's typical for children of alcoholic families to assume an adaptive role in the family that helps them to cope. He describes those roles as "maladaptive behavior". But the bottom line is that children, no matter the circumstance, find a way to survive. We humans are resilient creatures. My way was to become the "Hero", a doer, and a perfectionist. Other roles are the Scapegoat, the Mascot, the Lost Child, the Enabler, and so on. Most likely, those of us that grow up in dysfunctional homes adopt various bits of those behaviors. Whatever it takes to carry on with living.

I learned at a young age how to take charge of myself and whatever I could around me. It was a way to manufacture an external sense of safety and control that I wasn't internally getting from my significant caretakers. Deep inside, it felt like I was standing on quicksand, constantly struggling to stay afloat. The alternative would be to succumb to the chaos and groundlessness that was reflective of that place I called home. Instinctively, I didn't want to be like that. Or be like them. I learned how to put on a good "face" for the outside world because to reveal the truth of our house of cards would be admitting how disgraced I felt.

The week I turned eighteen, I moved out of my family home. I had a car and was gigging enough to pay rent and take care of myself. I didn't look back for a long time, except for some major holidays. I wanted to get as far away from my family and those feelings of pain and deprivation as I could. But in fact, my family ghosts followed me wherever I went. I think, too, that my leaving home when I did left my younger brother and sister feeling abandoned. I think they all felt a sense of resentment toward me for pursuing a life beyond the contracted existence we grew up with. They felt I was arrogant and uncaring toward them and told me so. As much as my parents, and my mother in particular, were proud of me, I believe deep down, my mother felt jealous that I went on to have the career that she had wanted. It left me to struggle for years with the idea that I had betrayed my family by going out into the world to create the life of my dreams. But by the grace of God or a higher power, I realized that I was born to survive… and even thrive.

Stranger in a Strange Land

"May you live in interesting times" - Fredric R. Coudert or interpretation of an old Chinese curse

Feeling out of place used to be my normal state of being. Like that odd piece of pottery you bought at a garage sale that doesn't really match your decor. I was always either the wrong color, shape, or size. Or maybe I was mistakenly dropped into the wrong time period. I don't know. At one point, I even thought I was adopted.

I could never really put my finger on the source of this unsettled, ungrounded sense I carried around with me when I was younger. But it was ever-present. Present as a low-lying cloud on a foggy day, looming like the ceiling of a small tent roof hanging over my head. Standing at 5' 7" by the time I hit the 6th grade, that feeling made me slouch. I always tried to keep myself inconspicuous. I felt contracted and recoiled into the feeling of "less than". Less white. Less smart. Less American. So I crouched and looked to the ground in order to not be noticed, which was nearly impossible. I stood out and up. Tall. Lanky. Dark hair and dark slanty eyes.

Growing up in the small, suburban, predominantly Anglo-Saxon, Catholic town of Wharton, New Jersey, it was a strange place to be. Being Eurasian, as I was identified then, felt painstakingly awkward. My family lived in a typical post-WWII American, middle-class neighborhood. No other kids or families around looked like me, my mother, or my older sister. It was pretty much a segregated white tract home neighborhood. Tract homes were prevalent constructions of the post-war economic boom of the fifties and sixties. All the houses looked the same, just like the people. White. A small faction of Latinos was in the neighboring town of Dover, but they were a scattered presence on the outskirts. Not mixed in.

Wharton was a nice little town, as towns go. It was quiet and clean. We had a decent house that my father could buy because of the GI Bill. It was one of the benefits of being a veteran then. My parents paid $16,000 for the house in 1960, which sounds cheap. But based on the value of money and the cost of living then, it was a typical middle-class house.

My mother, being full-blooded Japanese and rudely christened a "war bride" back then, was sentenced to the fate of being an outcast, too. I don't think my mother ever came to terms with that label or her newly adopted station in life. The only bit of saving grace was that our area was basically a New York City bedroom community. My father traveled daily by train to NYC for work, so it was politically a little more progressive than if we had landed somewhere in the Deep South.

My older sister Miyuki, or Miki for short, was also challenged by the strange new environment we were transported into. Because she couldn't speak English very well, the school system didn't know what to do with her. They didn't have English as a second language programs then. So, at the age of thirteen, they put her in the third or fourth grade until she caught up with her language skills. I'm sure that must have been arduous for her, though she says it wasn't that bad.

Going off to kindergarten was another torturous, separation anxiety-ridden event for me. I remember crying uncontrollably those first days of school. During my elementary school years I was sent to St. Mary's Catholic School in Wharton. That, too, felt like further punishment. I was forced to trade in my kimono and zori for a blue plaid uniform and saddle shoes. I remember it feeling like I had been issued a prison jumpsuit. I didn't like it there. I was naive to the ways of America and Catholic schools. I felt as though I was made to feel guilty for everything. But that is the goal of Catholicism, isn't it? We're all sinners. So we should feel guilty. Everyone has to pay for the "original sin" of Adam and Eve, who I believe were set up to fail by an unforgiving god. We humans simply aren't perfect. God punished everyone quite a bit in those Bible stories. I always thought he was kind of mean, considering we were created in his image. But he got what he set out to do. He made his followers fearful and obedient, like every other power-hungry leader. Shall I tell you more about how I feel about organized religion?

It was difficult as a five-year-old to make sense of these heady thrashings of crime and punishment. I felt labeled a criminal, erroneous, a foreigner, and struggled to recover from the hang-over of my trans-pacific, trans-cultural seismic shift.

Being born into an exotic, mysterious culture, salty, earthy food, and with an almost alien language to me now, my young mind couldn't figure out why I was surrounded by all these strange-looking people. My soul was imprinted with indelible pictures and ideas of what my life should look like. And America wasn't it. With the original building blocks of my personality stripped away, I was left with little to stand on. My identity and cultural branding before the age of four disappeared. Just like the magic tablecloth trick. Or like the Rotor ride at the amusement park, where the floor drops away beneath you, and you're glued to the wall by centrifugal force. I was groundless.

It would take me many years of therapy to understand that I was living with a broken heart, and a deep well of loneliness and sadness. As an adult, I realized that my mother and perhaps my older sister suffered with those feelings too. They just never knew how to express it.

That original sin in my life kicked off a chain of traumas. Like Adam and Eve, I felt like I was set up. As if God, or whoever was in charge, had laid out this obstacle course for me and rolled the dice. It felt like a nasty game show, but a challenge I vowed to take on. I was going to figure out how to survive and, in fact, thrive.

Underneath the rubble of raw emotional upset, there has always been a fireball of energy in my belly pushing me forward. And no matter how wrecked I felt inside, I wasn't going to let the outside world know. I committed myself to looking like I was ok… saving face. And no matter how awkward and out of place I felt, I would find a way to fit in and belong. Or create my own special identity space in the world as a stranger in this strange land.

My Musical DNA

"Music was my refuge. I could crawl into the space between the notes and curl my back to loneliness" - Maya Angelou

I remember my mother always singing or playing music when I was young. Whether it was the radio, records, or musicals on TV... my mother loved music. And though our house was shrouded in the dark drone of a typical dysfunctional alcoholic family, music soothingly seeped through the cracks of that suffocation and promised a glimmer of hope. It was evident that there was a life outside the walls of the despair we lived in.

My mother was the descendant of a very musical family. My grandfather was a strict classical musician. He was a graduate of the Tokyo University of the Arts and taught there as well. He instructed choirs, and taught piano and general music education. I believe he was highly esteemed in his circles and did quite well in his time. My grandmother, Chie Komatsu Sasaki, was also a graduate of the College of Arts, as were my Aunt Chizuko and Uncle Kaoru.

My mother was the eldest child of four children and the only girl. I think to this day, that's considered a big family in Japan. There were three younger brothers: Kazuya, Kaoru, and Michiya. My grandfather saw to it that they all trained in music as children. As a result, they all pursued careers in music in some capacity.

The eldest brother, Kazuya, as I understand it, ended up as a master tuner for the Yamaha piano manufacturing plant. He was able to repair various instruments. I remember him as a shy but warm person. I don't remember his wife. Kazuya died from heart failure alone in his home after his wife had passed away from a protracted illness. I think he died of a broken heart.

Kaoru played saxophone and loved Big Band music and Oscar Peterson. His son, my cousin Akio, told me once that his father actually wanted to be a violinist. Kaoru played in jazz bands as a saxophonist. He told me once that his challenge was getting away from the score and being able to improvise. He had a fascination with jazz and the freedom of expression it offers. It's such a familiar struggle for many classically trained musicians - to be free of the written page, and play strictly from the heart and imagination. I remember Kaoru to be funny and sweet with me whenever I visited Japan.

The youngest brother, Michiya, whom I never got to meet, became a very good composer. I'm told he even attended Columbia University in New York for a short period to study composition. Unfortunately, he died at the young age of 32 from stomach cancer. Sadly, he would never get to see his career to fruition. His wife, my Aunt Machiko, was a wonderful person who lived into her nineties and never remarried. Machiko was a kind and intelligent woman. She was always warm and generous with me when I visited Japan. We occasionally kept in touch over the years. My mother and Machiko kept in touch frequently through the years, up until my mother became ill and suffered from dementia and depression. Machiko's son was and still is a Buddhist priest. And he remains a caretaker of a temple in Tokyo.

My mother was the first child of her family. I'm sure there were parenting skills tried out on her that were later discarded. From my mother's account, when she was a little girl, my grandfather tried to teach her piano. He was a tough disciplinarian. And back in the 1930s, it wasn't uncommon for parents to hit their children with or without an implement like a ruler or a switch. Even when I was young, my father used a leather belt to discipline me. Nonetheless, according to my mother, when she made mistakes or played poorly during her piano lessons with her father, he would smack her on the side of her head. The thrust of the impact of his hand would set her spinning around atop the old-style round piano stool. Her little legs were dangling in the air, and her spirit was humiliated and hurt. My mother quickly developed a dislike for playing the piano.

My grandfather's harsh approach to teaching ultimately turned her off to classical music altogether.

Thanks to the support of her mother, my mother went on as a teenager to pursue singing, dancing, and theater. She attended the NHK Theater School in Tokyo, where all-female casts performed all the roles in various types of shows. From what I know of her stories and pictures, she was quite good. And she even had a little fan club. It explains why my mother, until the day she died, loved watching old Fred Astaire, Ginger Rogers, and Gene Kelly movies. It was her joy and escape from reality. Just as music became a sanctuary for me.

By the time WWII arrived in Japan, my mother, who was married to her first husband, a Japanese actor, and their child Miyuki, were sent in search of safety north of Tokyo. Many fled the cities during the war, just as is happening in Ukraine as I write. At the end of the war, she returned to Tokyo. By then, the landscape and timbre of the country had drastically changed. Japan surrendered, unable to fight against the brutality and devastation of the atom bombs that hit Hiroshima and Nagasaki. The country was taken over and occupied by the American military. It was a very different Japan. It was being controlled and Westernized.

As life in Japan slowly started to unfold into its new normal, my mother decided to pursue her singing career, performing American jazz standards and show tunes. It was the perfect repertoire for the new occupants of her homeland. And it fulfilled my mother's fantasies of escaping into the images of Hollywood movies, along with the stars of the glamorous forties musicals. I think those were probably some of my mother's happiest times in life.

My mother did various night club and supper club gigs in and around the Tokyo area. Her stage name was Peggy Futabu, as I remember. She took the American name "Peggy" in honor of Peggy Lee, whom she adored. Dressed in glamorous, custom-made, western-style dresses and gowns, she worked as a featured singer in various ensembles. One of her regular spots was singing at the Seamen's Service Club, located on the Army base in Yokohama. My father just so happened to be the residing manager in charge of this exclusive scene, where my parents would begin their romance.

According to my mother, once they started dating, my father would take her out dancing after their work at the club. They would go out on the town to late-night places, eat, drink, and carry on. It sounded very romantic. I imagine their nights to be a gentler version of what I experienced in NYC in the 1970s and 1980s. Perhaps it wasn't quite as debauched since my mother never took to drinking alcohol. As for many Asians, it didn't agree with her chemistry, flushing her face beet red with just one sip.

I imagine that during that time, my mother was swept away by this young, handsome American soldier in his crisp khaki uniform, like the thousands of Japanese women who eventually became war brides and US immigrants. They were young, naive, and painfully impressionable.

Like my mother, all the Japanese women who fell in love with American servicemen seemed to have had this idealized, Hollywood image of America as the land of plenty, where dreams come true, and life is perpetually beautiful. A place where women were adorned in glamorous gowns and jewels, and men were dashingly handsome in tailored suits and fedoras. They had little idea about the reality of what the future in America would be, once they crossed that line into the intercontinental, interracial, intercultural crossroad never before bridged. Life would never be the same. Nor would the world.

My mom and dad dating   Their Japanese wedding

My mom singing in the Seaman's Officer's Club on the
Army base in Yokohama

Music: My North Star

"In the midst of winter, I finally learned that there was in me an invincible summer" - Albert Camus

I knew from an early age that music would be very important to me. It would serve as my North Star, leading me to some kind of path in life. And perhaps even bring me fulfillment and happiness. Growing up in an unhappy home, I had little guidance. There was no operating manual or survival kit on how to be a functioning, well-rounded human in the world. Honestly, I lacked any sense of security, or the grasp that my parents really loved me. I felt pretty rudderless and unsafe most of my childhood. Though I know they loved me and my siblings in their own way, they were just so stunted and damaged from their own unhealed traumas that they simply lacked the ability to be stable, loving parents.

My mother, being Japanese and of the WWII generation, had her own complex inner world. She was quite stoic, generally undemonstrative, and emotionally contracted and cloaked. But the "face" she presented to the world was all smiles, never letting on about the truths of what life was like behind closed doors. Truthfully, her basic nature was one of truly kind generosity, and fortunately her love and talent for music, art, nature, gardening, and other admirable qualities softened her edges and served as a conduit to connect through.

My father was kind of a typical Depression baby man, a WWII vet, who was like an Archie Bunker character. He was macho, bigoted, minimally educated, and emotionally unavailable. And to top it off, his alcoholism arrested his personal development and any potential that lay hidden in his soul. But that said, he too loved music and having a good time. And somehow he saw past the irony of my mother's ethnicity and fell in love with her beauty enough to marry her; a person of color, a foreigner, the enemy, a Jap.

As an adult and after a lot of work on myself, I certainly no longer blame my parents for their shortcomings. It's just the way it was. However, in order to escape the depressing nature of my home life, music and fantasy were my friends. What better way to disassociate and channel one's pain than through a creative outlet? Or with drugs and alcohol. Or both.

From the time I was about eight or nine years old, I was singing in school and church. Somehow, I managed to score myself some featured vocal solos in the St Mary's church choir. I also participated in school talent shows and musicals. That's where I was introduced to the intoxicating rush of accolades running through my veins. How I loved that euphoric sensation when people complimented me about my voice. It made me feel warm and wanted. I felt validated and as though I was someone who had something of value to offer. I had no idea, at that age, about how that adoration would bolster my fractured sense of self. And more importantly, how it would serve as a healing salve for my tattered heart. It felt good.

During those elementary school years, I started singing at weddings, funerals, school functions, and any other occasion that presented itself. I discovered the power of having talent that gave me purpose and meaning. And I discovered I could make money from it. I was hooked! It was a potent, addictive elixir.

By the time I hit 8th grade, I had already been listening to everyone from the Beatles to the Rolling Stones, Joni Mitchell, Sly and the Family Stone, and Stevie Wonder, to name a few. All those iconic artists associated with the Summer of Love were a bright beacon of hope in my life.

I think the first song I learned how to play on guitar and sing was 'The House of the Rising Sun' by the Animals. Then Beatles and Joni Mitchell songs followed. I grew a deep passion for Joni Mitchell and her music, so much so that she became my muse and a role model for some time.

I was enchanted by the counterculture. I cheered the progressive movements that were bubbling up via that scene. (Not much has actually changed for me politically.) I loved the unconventional fashion. I loved the unruly attitudes. And I was intrigued by the attraction to spirituality. In many ways, it was East meets West... like me. There was something about the rebellious spirit of the anti-establishment movement that spoke to me. It resonated with how I felt about being in the middle of the white, middle-class, suburban community I was living in. The counterculture felt sexy, seductive, and a little dangerous. But it also inspired hope for a better future for everyone. Overall, it promised me a sense of belonging to a group, adopting an identity filled with freaks and social mutants. I found my tribe.

I listened to a lot of FM radio back then, which originated out of NYC. I recall WNEW in particular. Radio stations and DJs were so entertaining and informative at that time. They were the gatekeepers to the music business world. They delivered an exciting heap of musical variety. They informed us listeners about various contemporary artists. They also gave credit to the side musicians on records. I remember how they read the liner notes from album covers on air (who does that anymore?). They reported information about the record labels. And they captivated my dreams about pursuing a way into the magic world of the "biz". FM radio was a brave new frontier in progressive radio. It was an exciting time. The music, the culture, the social norms, the consciousness of life, and the landscape of a rapidly changing world: there was a kind of rarified atmosphere surrounding that orbit that I wanted to be a part of. I felt like Alice in Wonderland, and I was going to go down that rabbit hole.

Radio programming in those days encompassed an eclectic mix of various music genres within one show. I remember hearing anyone from Frank Sinatra to the Rolling Stones within the course of an hour on one program. I recall DJs like Vin Scelsa, Dennis Elsas, Carol Miller, Alison Steele, Pat St. John, Jonathan Schwartz, and Scott Muni. They would expound endlessly about the lives of the artists. They would explore cryptic meanings behind the lyrics of songs and take you on a journey. Anyone growing up in the NYC metro area at that time knew who these mavericks were. They were like the rock stars of the airwaves in the tri-state area.

I spent hours in my bedroom as a young teenager, listening to the radio, spinning records, plotting about what records I would buy next. I was a loner. I practiced singing in front of the mirror, and dreamt about being on stage with a band. There, in the bubble of my room, I taught myself to play guitar, and started to dabble in songwriting. My room and the music were my sacred space, and my sanity.

Shortly into my teenage musical explorations, I learned how to play and sing enough songs so I could venture out and explore playing gigs. I played as a solo act, starting in grammar school and becoming increasingly more active throughout high school. I think one of my first professional gigs was in a club called the Final Exam in Randolph, NJ. I played on an off night in the lounge with a guitar player named Ted Smith. I was thirteen or fourteen. I still have a cassette recording of that gig!

Not only did I play coffee house gigs, but I started to work in bands as well. I have hazy memories of competing with a band in a Battle of the Bands event in the high school gymnasium. I actually don't remember if we won. But I can summon the feeling of how much fun it was singing Black Sabbath, Jethro Tull, and Janis Joplin songs, wearing a black cape, and mimicking the cover of the Black Sabbath record. The band I was with bravely performed the song 'Black Sabbath'. It was laughably theatrical. It was completely out of my vocal range, and incongruous to the nature of my style, but no-one seemed to care. It was still cool. The excitement of thrashing guitars, bombastic drums, and the whirling reverb of the high school gym was trippy. The visceral sensation of those early band performances spoke to my teenage rebellious angst, and fed my fantasies. Those moments were hugely influential to the direction of my future. I knew in my gut that this was what I wanted to do: sing, perform, express myself through music, and see the world.

As my passion for this pathway in life blossomed, I began seeking out a community with more and more musicians. Most of them were older boys with cars. All of them with long hair, holey jeans, and a look that has now become expensive high-fashion vogue. Running with an older crowd, I started smoking pot and drinking alcohol around the age of fourteen, which is hard for me to fathom now. I started doing more and more gigs and getting entrenched in a hippie kind of lifestyle. Meanwhile, my parents thought I was just into music, which was true. However, there was a wilder side to my life outside the house that they were oblivious to. Nor did they seem to take much interest in knowing. They were myopically caught up in their own orbit and problems.

In my freshman year of high school, I hung out with a group of kids who were the "hippies" of our school. They were all a little older than me. There was a guy named Martin, who was really cute and smart. I recall him being kind of the centerpiece of this group. They hung out a lot on the Morris Hills High School front lawn during lunch breaks and after school. Some people smoked pot out there. Some of us had guitars and played music and sang. It was for me where the "cool" kids were.

In 1971, there was a big anti-Vietnam War demonstration being planned in Washington D.C. The cool kids were planning on going. And they were going to drop acid. I was fifteen. It sounded dangerously fun, and I wanted to be a part of this historical event. There was no way my parents would agree to let me go if they knew the truth. So I told them I was spending the weekend with a girlfriend. Off I went with these older kids on a road "trip" to D.C.

When we arrived in the Washington area, I just remember the excitement of seeing swarms of "freaks" walking the streets. They were our tribesmen. I recall how difficult it was to find a parking space. And I remember being worried that it might be hard to find our car later. After we got settled, we found a place to sit in a park somewhere, where we all dropped some "orange sunshine". I remember being scared, but being intrigued by what the experience would be like. I told Martin I was a little afraid, so he gave me half of the barrel-shaped pill. We all hung close together. I hung close to Martin.

As the drug came on, I remember feeling this terrible sense of uneasiness and fear. It was the first time I was experiencing a breakdown of my ego and persona. At that point, I was so insecure and damaged that my psyche was overwhelmed with the internal identity struggle brought on by the LSD. I know now that I was too young to be doing that stuff. I can vaguely conjure the sense of terror I felt then, and the vision of me hanging on to Martin's jacket for dear life. I was like a child holding on to their parent's hand for security. He didn't seem to mind. And if he did, he never told me.

I didn't know how to process that experience back then. In retrospect, I see now that my mind made a radical shift in consciousness. It opened the door to the inner workings of the core of my being. It acquainted me with the tender, broken area in my heart that had been there all along, that seemed to contain answers to so many questions. It revealed that I unconsciously knew the answers, but I didn't know how to approach unraveling it all at that age. That core of questions is the same spot I would revisit time and time again in therapy, and in my personal work over the years. It was there to teach me about the real nature of reality and my soul, but this student wasn't quite ready for those lessons back then.

That first acid trip, in the middle of thousands of people at an anti-war demonstration, would not be the way I would recommend for anyone, especially someone so young, to have an experience like that. I know now that the set and setting, and with whom you do that kind of work, are so important.

I'm grateful that we survived that experience safe and sound. I'll never forget the images of that march against the war, and the impassioned cries of the demonstrators, which included soldiers who had come back from Vietnam. It made a big impression on me that they were speaking out, particularly with my father being a military guy. The whole experience cracked open my beliefs about the state of the world, the impact of the war, and the truth about the changing society and politics around me. But what I remember most was the discovery of a deeper sense, another level of consciousness. There was no turning away from that. I would never be the same.

As I approached the age of sixteen, I wanted nothing more than to get out of high school and start living the life of a bohemian, working musician in a band. I never felt like I jibed with high school kids. I had very few friends my own age. Most of my friends were actually out of school. So, in my junior year of high school, I initiated a plan with the school administration to graduate early. Consequently, I asked my parents to sign a letter giving me permission to graduate at the end of my junior year. They shockingly agreed. I knew what I wanted to do, and school was not going to be the place to do it. College, at that point, seemed useless to me. Even though I was accepted into Berklee College of Music, my parents couldn't afford to pay for college because of my father's gambling debts and the hardships they were embroiled in. But at the time, it was fine with me.

So in 1973, I graduated a year ahead of schedule, not because I was so damn smart, but because I was lucky enough to know what I wanted to do, what my passion was, and where I wanted to go. I was determined to be a professional singer and musician, and nothing would stop me.

From the Music Box to Julep Joints

"The beginning is the most important part of the work" – Plato

After graduating high school, I took a job working in the now legendary music store The Music Box, in Ledgewood, NJ. The proprietor, Tom Barth, was a strikingly handsome guy and a truly kind soul. I had previously met Tom when I was thirteen years old, when his store was located in the nearby town of Dover. It's where I bought guitar strings and musical supplies, and where I discovered all the local musicians hung out. As I became friendlier with Tom and his then wife Barbara, I eventually became the babysitter for their young daughter Tara.

By the time I was sixteen and graduating from high school, Tom had moved to the bigger location in Ledgewood, NJ. I guess since I had proven I was trustworthy as a babysitter, he hired me to be the "behind-the-counter girl" in the store. I loved working at The Music Box. It was such a cool meeting place for musicians near and far, amateur and professional. I met many players of all sorts, and started threading together my little New Jersey network. The Music Box was the go-to place if you were in the market for all sorts of musical gear, but particularly unique vintage guitars, and repair work on instruments of all sorts. Tommy was very knowledgeable and capable as a self-taught technician.

Tom was actually a pioneer in the world of vintage guitars in the early 1970s. People like Ricky Metlock of the band Blackfoot and later of Lynyrd Skynyrd bought guitars from him. And as Tom's reputation overflowed into the collectors' circles, Bruce Springsteen and Paul McCartney were also known to have purchased guitars from him. Later, Tom partnered with Bob

Benedetto, a renowned luthier and jazz guitarist in the area, and together they designed Tom's signature line of guitars called the Barth Vader and the Tommy Hawk. I'm not sure how successful his line of guitars was, but I'm sure they were fun to play and sounded great.

I learned so much from Tom about guitars, musical instruments and being a good human. Tom was a living example of having passion for the things you love, and the importance of a connection to community. He loved guitars, musicians, his family, and being of service. He lived his life with great enthusiasm for all those things, and he made a difference in the lives of many.

Sadly, Tom died way too young, in 2005, at the age of fifty-five, from pancreatic cancer. The last time I saw him, at a benefit concert organized to help with his medical expenses, he was still incredibly handsome and full of smiles and warmth. I remember as I was leaving the event and hugging him, I thought to myself, how can someone so good looking and sweet be so sick? It seemed such a cruel and unfair punishment from the universe, or god, or whoever's in charge.

I'll never forget Tom, his beautiful spirit, and the marvelous opportunity he gave me early in life, which led me to the next important stepping stone on my musical journey.

While working at The Music Box, I met a crazy character of a guitar player and singer named Grover Kemble. At the time, Grover was a member of a popular local band called The Everyman Band. They were a funky, eclectic group of wild and woolly musicians who could get everybody up and dancing, while displaying a high level of musicianship, in and around small clubs in the NJ/NY metro area. I thought they were some of the best players around at the time. They were made up of drummer Michael Suchorsky, bassist Bruce Yaw, saxophonist Marty Fogel, guitarist David Torn and Grover on lead vocals and guitar. Later, in the 70s, they went on to be the back-up band for Lou Reed for several years, minus Grover and David. The Everyman Band ended up making a few notable records for the ECM label and left their unique brand of music in the jazz fusion world and the New Jersey music scene.

Grover Kemble was, and still is, the consummate frontman who entertains an audience much like a circus barker leading you into the big tent to see the secret spectacle inside. A fabulous flaunt and flirt, he could win anyone over with his self-effacing charm and humor. It was always a fabled night anytime you went to see him in whatever band he played with. He knew how to bring performances alive with his vaudevillian-style banter and clown-like physical gestures. I often thought that he was born in the wrong era with his personality. If you can imagine a kind of rock 'n' roll Jimmy Durante, then you have an idea of his style. He surely would have been hugely successful in that vaudevillian era.

While working at The Music Box, I started following Grover and the Everyman Band. I was smitten by his goofy charm and musical distinction. Soon after, I started taking guitar lessons with him. One thing led to another, and I started dating him. Then, we started making music together professionally as a duo. It's probably not how I would recommend developing a career now, but c'est la vie. I was young.

A few years into working as a duo, Grover and I developed a respectable following and started building a consistent momentum of gigs and a steady income stream, to such an extent that I was able to buy a brand-new car and move into an apartment on my own by the time I was eighteen years old. Unfortunately, the Chevy Vega I bought had an aluminum engine that blew up the week I made my last loan payment.

As the momentum and our fan base grew, we decided to expand our ensemble with the addition of a rhythm section. According to Dave Miller, our bass player, he and Tim Solook, who had already been playing together as a unit, caught a rumor that Grover and I were looking to expand into a band. They decided to check us out at one of our regular weekly gigs at the Publick House in Chester, NJ. After a friendly post-gig conversation, we jammed together the following week, and the rest is history, as they say.

The chemistry between musicians is a mysterious thing. You either have it or you don't. It's like the conversation I've had many times with my husband and other musicians about "groove" or "pocket". It's all about how people feel the rhythm or musical time. That's not to say many musicians don't have good time; it's more about how they "feel" the time. And the concept of the pocket is not necessarily something you can teach. To me, it's an inherent inner clock that a musician is born with. You know it when you hear it and feel it. It just is. So when Dave, Tim, Grover and I got together, it was Cinderella's shoe that fit perfectly.

From the first time Grover, Dave, Tim, and I played together, we just kind of knew that it was going to work. Our personalities neatly meshed, and our "feel" for the music jelled instantly. Most importantly, Dave and Tim liked having fun and entertaining a crowd, which was of great importance to Grover and me. Thus Grover, Margret & Za Zu Zaz was born.

In case you're wondering, we chose the name Za Zu Zaz for the band because swing, vocal bebop, and jazz pop was a part of our eclectic repertoire. Cab Calloway had recorded a song with that title in 1933. It exemplified the fun scat vocal style that he popularized. And we wanted to embody his brand of energetic, stylish entertainment with how we performed. It was a formula that helped us to successfully stand out in the myriad of bands in a booming club scene at that time. And my mother, being an Anglophile, had given me Margaret as my birth name, honoring Princess Margaret of England. I just shortened it a bit so it looked better on the posters and our drummer's kick drum cover.

After a couple of years of enjoying our dynamic foursome, we decided to expand our sound with one more layer by adding a keyboard player. That's when John Gatti entered the picture. John had been a member of a well-known NY area rock band named The Good Rats. I think we caught him right when he was ready for a musical change. Luckily for us, John was just the right person to bring the joy and musical spice that sparked our already beautifully cohesive blend.

G, M, & ZZZ had an extraordinarily successful run playing every major club in the NJ/ NY metropolitan area. We developed a reputation notable enough to be invited to play the Spoletto Jazz Festival, Newport Jazz Fest, The Bottom Line in NYC, and The Roxy in LA, to name just a few brag-worthy gigs. For a period of time we had great management with a man named Mort Lewis. Mort had managed Simon and Garfunkel and was instrumental in their early success, as well as other artists. We came incredibly close to a major record deal and taking that next step in our careers. But due to the time period, the changing record industry, and our eclectic, unique sound, it just never panned out.

Overall, we proudly developed our organization to a high professional level; owning our sound system and lights, owning a truck, and employing a small crew that traveled with us everywhere. We were the little engine that could, proudly making a living making music, and having the time of our lives.

Za Zu Zaz had a uniquely eclectic, hybrid brand of jazz, swing, and jazz fusion music. We were all accomplished instrumentalists, and demonstrated strong vocal harmonies. We were entertaining and made a lot of people happy. Our multi flavored blend of music was our strength. But at the same time, it was most likely our downfall. Record industry people loved us, but had a hard time labeling what we did. So they passed.

The mid/late 1970s was coming out of the Vietnam War-era-fueled music of protest, Civil Rights, Women's lib, psychedelia, consciousness-raising, and a lot of internal soul searching that needed to happen through the 60s and 70s. So when you look at the popular musical landscape, we went from Bobby Darin and Anette Funicello in bobby socks and bikinis, to the Beatles, Elvis, and the Stones, with long-haired hippies, drugs, and Eastern philosophy. The logical step from there was going to be a place completely different. So the hippy music turned into punk, and the new bobby socks became padded shoulders and sequins with disco music. Then there was everything in between… like us. We were at the dawn of MTV, videos and the development of the computer/internet age that would change the world.

In hindsight, it was an amazing musical training ground for me that could not be paralleled by even the best universities in the world. It was real-life experience that not only made me a good musician, singer, and performer but also helped me develop a true sense of confidence in my talent.

At the end of a productive, amazing run with Grover and the band, I gave notice in 1980 that I was leaving. It broke up the band as it was and broke the guys' hearts, especially Grover's. But I needed to move on in search of grander dreams and to grow.

That incredibly instructive and successful period of my early career, of working four to five nights a week in clubs, concert halls and festivals, helped me to cultivate practical musical and professional skills in ways that nothing else could. The influence of that background served to equip me with what I needed for future work, enduring even to this day.

I will forever be grateful to that band and that experience with that group. It was a special and formidable time in my life with those boys, especially with Grover. He was a mentor and great supporter of my talents… maybe even kind of a father figure to me. Those memories and my lifelong friendships with them will forever be a part of my life.

On May 31st, 2025, G, M, and ZZZ performed together for the last time at a reunion concert at The Tabernacle in Mt. Tabor, NJ. We performed to a sold-out show of old and new fans, revisiting our unique blend of jazz bebop vocal tunes from Lambert, Hendricks and Ross, Cab Calloway, and others, as well as some old and new original songs. It was a sweetly nostalgic and fantastic night that stirred up many great memories for us and our fans. The outpouring of love and support was tremendous and so gratifying.

S

Grover, Margret & Za Zu Zaz 1979

Pop: Rhythmic Quartet

By JOHN S. WILSON

ALTHOUGH the stylistic basis for Grover Margret and Za-Zu-Zaz, a quartet that appeared at the Other End on Tuesday evening, is primarily the tight, rhythmic, jump style of Louis Jordan and his Tympany Five and the King Cole Trio, before Nat Cole shifted his emphasis to ballad singing, the group reaches out in so many other directions that it has the potential for presenting a performance that could be dazzling and exhilarating in its variety and changes of pace.

That it is not quite that is because some parts of their material are less dazzling than others. The quartet — Grover Kemble and Margret Taylor, who play guitars and sing; Dave Miller, a bassist who often adds a third voice, and Tim Solook, a drummer who is occasionally a fourth voice — create tight, full vocal blends that, backed by their electric instruments, can capture the sound and spirit of the swing band in full flight on "Jersey Bounce" or turn to the crisp, staccato phrasing of be-bop. They mix their jump tunes with mood pieces, Latin rhythms, original ballads and an overlay of high, penetrating, twangy guitar playing.

Miss Taylor, a striking-looking Eurasian, has an even more striking voice that she warms up with some adept scat singing, and eventually explodes in a display of vocalizing that takes off in the Yma Sumac manner. Mr. Kemble, a modest and unpretentious singer, is more concerned with guitar solos that become rather monotonous and set a shrill tone that does not sit well with the warmth and depth of the group's ensemble singing.

Despite the variety of the group's sources, there is a surprising lack of variety in much of their performance that comes largely from the monotony of their instrumental sound. Miss Taylor's virtuoso vocalizing gets them away from that sound, and so does their ensemble singing. If they could find some other means of varying it, the razzle-dazzle that is now potential might become real.

The New York Times
Published: December 21, 1978
Copyright © The New York Times

Our 45th year reunion gig May 2025

51

All Aboard!

"Life is a train that stops at no stations: You either jump aboard, or stand on the platform and watch as it passes" - Yasmina Khadra

After leaving Za Zu Zaz, I had a short stint with another local band, appropriately called Splat. It didn't amount to much except for a few gigs and some nice local reviews, leaving me feeling more confused about my future. Also at that time, my year-or-so-long relationship with trumpeter Randy Brecker sadly ended. So I was a completely free agent looking for a new plan.

Since Zaz had been booked by the Willard Alexander Agency in NYC, I turned to them for advice. Willard Alexander was a legendary booking agent who helped usher in the Big Band era with groups like Benny Goodman, the "King of Swing". Among Mr. Alexander's other clients were bands led by Maynard Ferguson, Buddy Rich, Arty Shaw, the Count Basie Band, the Duke Ellington Orchestra, Guy Lombardo, Tony Dorsey, Jimmy Dorsey, The Russ Morgan Orchestra, and The Glenn Miller Orchestra. He kept all those bands working for years, some well beyond their prime. Later, he booked what was known as "ghost bands"… the bands of the leaders who had died, leaving them with a famous book of music and a substantial fan base. The Glenn Miller Orchestra was one of those "ghost bands".

Since Glenn died in 1944 in a plane crash during the war, the longevity of the band was purely based on the book of memorable songs from that era. It just so happened that in 1981 when I was looking for a gig, they were looking for a new female singer.

Wayne Hutchinson, who was Zaz's agent, set up an audition with the band and then band leader, trombonist Larry O'Brien. I got the gig.

Traveling with the Glenn Miller Orchestra was training for road life 1940s style. The band traveled on a standard Greyhound bus of the day, with all the seats intact. Each member of the band got their allotted two seat "area". That was your space: your closet, your bed, your private island. The band was made up of nineteen guys and me. One of the sax players, Dick Gerhardt, doubly served as a tour manager. Many times, Dick had his wife with him assisting. They somehow managed with sharing a two seat space; I don't know how they did it, but I think a fair amount of vodka was involved.

Being in my twenties and having had a lot of work experience under my belt already, I felt prepared to hit the road and work at that level of intensity. But in reality, the tour scheduling was quite insane. Like many bands on the road then and now, they would have to work at least four to six nights a week, in a different city each night, to make the business profitable. I felt like the show schedule was patterned after a dartboard game played by drunks. Be that where they land.

A typical tour schedule would go something like this: do a show in one city, get on the bus after the show. That's called a "hit and run". The driver would drive most of the night to the next town while you slept sitting up or hunched over sideways across your two-seat sanctuary. Generally, we'd arrive in the wee hours of the morning in the next city and slither off the bus in a mid-sleep stupor. Then, in that zombie state, we'd check into the new hotel, get a few more hours of sleep, get up, and shit, shower, and shave, as the boys would say. Mid/late afternoon, we'd usually roll down to the lobby for call time and drift to the venue as a collective pod. Band members were the roadies too, so some members would schlep gear and set up the show. By soundcheck, most everyone was awake and warming up to perform. The venue would usually serve dinner of some kind. We'd miraculously slog through the show, and then get on the bus to do the whole spin cycle over again. Needless to say, touring life, even in the most elite and high class circumstances, is a grind.

Being the featured female vocalist in the band, much of my job was to be an accoutrement of sorts. Gary Martin, the male vocalist, and I would sit down stage left in chairs right in front of the band. Make no mistake, sitting on stage is work in a very different way. We still had to be "on". We would sit and smile at the band and the audience, pretending we were really enjoying ourselves, being eye candy. When it was our time to step up to the mic, which wasn't very often, we'd have to turn on our song and dance routine center stage and be the center of attention. It was torturous some nights just sitting there, smiling, trying to look happy when I was bored out of my mind. I think it's much harder not singing when you're on stage, rather than being busy working. But in keeping with the tradition of the Big Band era style, singers were not the main part of the show. They were a side dish; a novelty, meant to spice things up without stealing the spotlight.

Nevertheless, I was very grateful for the opportunity to learn about singing in the Big Band context, and working with a director in that way. Larry O'Brien was a wonderful band leader and a consummate gentleman. I learned a great deal about arrangements for Big Band music. I heard some great young, up and coming players in that band too. Many of them were just out of college and on fire. Being in that environment educated my ears with a deeper understanding about jazz harmony, dynamics, and how a music machine like a Big Band needs to co-operate in order to sound like a unified entity. These were things that college could have given me, but I was living it. And I got to sing some beautiful arrangements of some classic songs like 'Tangerine', 'I Got it Bad', 'Don't Sit Under the Apple Tree', 'Pennsylvania 6,5000' and of course 'In the Mood'. It was a sweet tasting of a musical era gone by. And a gift of a lifetime to have had that unique experience, however brief.

The biggest bonus of working with that band was that it took me back to Japan for the first time as an adult. I was able to reunite with my grandfather, aunts, uncles and cousins after almost twenty years of not seeing them. Unfortunately, my grandmother had died several years before that. So I never saw her again. But it was a thrill to re-establish a bit of a relationship with my family in Japan.

I'm happy to say that I'm still in touch with my cousin Akio to this day.

How strange it must have been for my family in Japan to see me return to them singing with a WWII-era big band, initially led by an American soldier. What a twist of fate for a little Japanese-American girl, singing the music Americans were dancing to while the military was plotting to drop the atom bomb on Japan. It's bizarre.

After about a year with the Glenn Miller Orchestra, I jumped ship with the piano player and landed in Tempe, Arizona. I lived with him and his parents for about a year, which in hindsight was a peculiar tangent in my life. I think it resonated with that part of me that was seeking a genuine family connection. Not surprisingly, I didn't find it there. However, I took a few classes at ASU and took a break from the road. Needless to say, it was a bit of a confusing time period. When I came to my senses I broke up that relationship, and headed back to New York City, where my heart and home were calling me to return.

Gary Martin, Me, Larry O'Brien and the GM Orchestra

Me & Rosemary Clooney

Tour Schedule 1981

GLENN MILLER ORCHESTRA

Contact: Willard Alexander, Inc.
660 Madison Avenue
New York, NY 10021
(212) 751-7070

Itinerary — June & July, 1981

Date	City	Venue	Time
10 Jun	Chicago, IL	Marriott Hotel	5 – 9 PM
11	Hinsdale, IL	Katherine Legge Memorial Park	8 – 10 PM
12	Northbrook, IL	Mission Hills C C	8:30 – 12:30 AM
13	Willow Springs, IL	Willowbrook Ballroom	9 – 1 AM
14	Kenosha, WS	University of Wisconsin	2 – 9 PM
15	Norwalk, OH	Town & Country Theatre	8 – 10 PM
16	Mt Sulpher Springs, WV	Greenbrier Hotel	8 – 12 mid
17			
18	Wayne, PA	Covered Wagon Inn	9 – 1 AM
19	Rhinbeck, NY	IBM – Dutchess Co fairgrounds	12 noon – 6 PM
20	Huntingdon, NY	PAF Playhouse	8 – 12 mid
21	Vacation – thru 28 Jun		
29	Chautauqua, NY	Chautauqua Institution	8:30 – 10:30 PM
30	Indianapolis, IN		
1 Jul			
2			
3	Vienna, VA	Wolftrap	8 – 12 mid
4	Chestertown, MD	Oaks Landing	9:30 – 1 AM
5	Toms River, NJ	Ocean Co Park	
6			
7			
8	Bradford, PA	Pepphills Club	8 – 12 mid
9	London, Ont	Wonderland	
10	Watertown, Ont	N.Wentworth C C	
11	Caledon Hills, Ont	Geo Gardiner Residence	
12			
13	Darien, CT	Darien Dinner Theatre	
14			
15	Bear Mtn, NY	Bear Mtn Inn	
16	Geneva, NY		

The **MILLER SOUND** lives forever!

The Jackson Victory Tour

"We cannot learn anything from inaction, so the only real failure is to never try at all" - Tony Robbins

I drove cross-country by myself back to NYC from Phoenix, a 2,409-mile ride. Immediately, I started reaching out to people I knew, looking for a place to live and work. An old friend, Jed DePhilipis, who had helped Za Zu Zaz back in the day, was working on the production crew with the Jackson Victory Tour. They were setting up a show at what was then called Giant Stadium in the Meadowlands in New Jersey.

The Jackson Victory Tour was a massive operation with a leapfrog stadium crew of over 250 people, 42 semi-trucks, and even a newspaper of its own called The Jacksonburg Picayune. It was the greatest and biggest production ever at the time. Michael Jackson was at the pinnacle of his career. And the brothers joining him on this show was the event of the year. In the long run, I think the tour didn't profit in the way the investors had predicted. But it was still a monumental event, chronicled in rock 'n' roll history.

When I spoke with Jed at the time, he said the tour was looking for a local production assistant who could work for the week. I was free and needed the money, so I jumped at the opportunity, even if it wasn't singing. Taking that leap ended up being an experience that forged long-time friendships and created connections that helped change my career's direction.

This is a prime example of what I advise my students now. You never know where life will lead you, and what opportunities will emerge from any given situation. So take every chance you can to make connections, work, make money, and embrace experiences that will help you develop the skills you might use down the line. It's all about learning and growing, especially in those early years. Certainly, this is a good philosophy for life in general. It turned out that working on that tour was such a fantastic gift of a lifetime, adding various tentacles to my business network.

That first week working in the production office was a whirling, buzzing rush of activity I had never witnessed before. Staging guys, riggers, lighting, sound crews, backline, security, and the chain of all the elements it takes to put on a show of that magnitude and stature. I hadn't had that depth of production knowledge until that point. Seeing how multi-layered and massive an effort it was, contrasted to my history of playing clubs and small concert halls, was eye-opening. It was production on steroids flexing big muscles. And I was getting an exclusive inside view of it all.

By the end of that first week at Giant Stadium, the intimidating and somewhat aloof production manager, Peyton Wilson, asked if I was available to travel on for the rest of the tour. I was pleasantly shocked and jumped at the opportunity. It gave me guaranteed work until the end of the year and possibly longer. What a relief.

When we hit the next show, at Madison Square Garden, a new woman came onboard to also assist in the production. Marcene Peterson. Marcene was a wild, vivacious, smart, blonde, rock 'n' roll chick, who had just spent years working with the band Heart. She was fresh off of being the personal assistant to Ann and Nancy Wilson in the late 70s and early 80s. It was at the peak of Heart's career, when they were having massive Billboard hits. Marcene was no stranger to touring life and big concert productions.

Marcene and I became fast friends. Being a few years older than me, she was like the big sister I never had. She was edgy, fun and bossy, but in a good way. As the younger pup, I was happy to follow in her footsteps. We had an easy rhythm to our production trailer workflow and were spirits simpatico. I was good at following directions and taking the initiative. We were organized, efficient, and fun. The friendly, flirty girls in the office. We worked hard, and partied hard, while keeping a behemoth of a show on track. Everyone loved coming into our trailer to see us. And, of course, we had the power of the backstage pass allotment, which was like gold.

After a long day of tasks, ensuring things were in order for that day's show, and prepping for the next, we would break out the cranberry juice and vodka every night around dinner time. After cocktails and dinner, a little bump of cocaine was usually dessert. It was the 80s after all. Cocaine was the raving drug of choice for most partiers back then. It flurried like snow all around us in that sphere. And as women, we could usually get a free hit from someone, even if we didn't have our own stash.

On show nights, during the show, we would take turns visiting the makeshift club setup under the stage that the crew guys fabricated. It was called Mr Lucky's. Lights were strung up under the scaffolding of the stage in a little maze-like setup, creating the fantasy of an exclusive underground club, which, for all intents and purposes, it was. It was a secret meeting place for people who didn't need to be actively working during the show, like us in production, riggers, truck drivers etc; even some of the back line guys would sneak down there occasionally. It was where you could imbibe whatever was around and socialize a bit with comrades. That clandestine happening was our entertainment while the Jackson Family passionately sang and gyrated over our heads on stage to the buzzing, screaming tens of thousands of people in the audience. If they only knew what was really happening behind the scenes - or underneath, as it was. I always wondered if Michael and the brothers knew what was going on in the underbelly of the beast. That said, they were probably just too preoccupied with the complexities of their own lives, which seemed quite dramatic. There appeared to be a lot going on behind the veil of their lives with the Jackson family at the time. From the production point of view, each brother had their own dressing room, limo, and entourage they traveled with, which I thought was odd, given they were family. And the parents were looming figures above all.

Looking back, all that crazy partying was nothing to envy. But the experiences, the sustained relationships with the wonderful people I met and worked with, being a part of one of pop music history's pivotal events, was a feather in my cap, with unforgettable memories.

A big take away for me was that I'm still close friends with Marcene, who later became Marcene O'Bryen. At the end of the Jackson Victory Tour, she got together with then Avalon Attractions production representative Danny O'Bryen. Avalon was one of the biggest West Coast concert promoters at the time next to Bill Graham, until it was sold to Live Nation in 1991. Danny, a hard-working, smart businessman with the soul of an artist, has since been very successful on his own with his company, Screenworks, providing big LED screens for big music and sporting events.

Marcene and Danny romantically rode off together into the sunset, in his sporty, white Datsun 280Z, at the end of the Jackson Victory Tour in December 1984. The next year, they married and have since raised two wonderful boys, who now have beautiful wives and children of their own. I'm so grateful that they're still a treasured part of my life.

Me & Michael Jackson end of tour party 1984

I Wanna Know What Love Is

"To reach a goal you've never before attained, you must do things you've never before done" - Richard Scott

1985 brought wildly unimagined experiences, such that when I look back now, I don't know how I survived it all.

In November 1984, Foreigner released their fifth studio album, Agent Provocateur. The lead single was their infamous power ballad, 'I Wanna Know What Love Is'. The song, for those of you that don't remember, featured a gospel choir and a female vocalist doing some wailing gospel riffs. In fact, it was Jennifer Holiday and the New Jersey Mass Choir, who were affiliated with the Gospel Music Workshop of America. Their contribution elevated the song to a heart-stirring, iconic anthem, making it the massive worldwide number one hit it became.

As the band was planning a world tour that would begin in early 1985, no one knew how they would pull off having a gospel choir spotlight their gold medal-winning song every night. It was impossible to carry a choir on tour, and organizing a local choir for every show all over the world had never been done before. They were at a loss.

Steve Nider, who remembered me from the Jackson Victory Tour production staff, knew I was a singer. He generously threw my name in the ring with Foreigner's manager Bud Prager. Bud, who also managed Leslie West and the band Mountain, along with other notables in the rock idiom, called me for an interview. Luckily, I was in NYC, where his office was located, and where the band was based.

I remember when I first met Bud in his ESP management office, his looming physical presence and brash, loud voice felt very intimidating. Sitting across from Bud at his seemingly gigantic desk, I realized he didn't know what to say to me about the job of organizing choirs at all. He had no idea how to instruct me, or anyone for that matter, on how to conquer this elephant of a mission. His lack of knowledge of what to tell me was so contrary to his overshadowing comportment and his shock of silver hair. So, without other options, he offered me the job on the spot if I wanted to take it on. I had no idea in that moment if I could do the job. And I had absolutely no concept of what I should be paid. But I just said yes. And I was hired.

I don't know how, but I've always had this embodied fearlessness, or naive optimism, guiding my compass. It has helped me maneuver through a lot of uncharted territory in life. Perhaps because of growing up feeling like a foreigner, and feeling less than, this little-yellow-girl in the white-man's-world complex, I always felt I needed to prove myself. Deep down, I needed validation from others to fill that empty, lonely space inside. I felt I needed to work harder to stake my place. Because I wasn't white and I was a woman, that meant that I had to do better to be accepted and be successful. So taking on what seemed an impossible task felt like a good challenge to prove my worth.

The ESP Management office was located at 1790 Broadway then. They offered me an office to start pre-production work for the upcoming worldwide tour. Worldwide? OMG! How was I going to book choirs in Japan? All over Europe? In Israel? What did I get myself into! There was no Google at the time. No internet for that matter. There were no laptop computers, for God's sake! All I had was this little room with a desk, a phone and a phone book. The rest was up to me to figure out. And I only had a few months before the tour started. Where the hell do I begin?

Luckily, because I went to Catholic school and sang in the church choir, I knew every church and university in the country would have a choir. But it had to be, preferably, a real gospel choir. Not just the run-of-the-mill "Anglo-Saxon" kind. So I began dialing the phone with the help of the Yellow Pages listings, 411 information, University listings, and paperbound directories I found for Baptist churches around the country. I made hundreds and hundreds of phone calls, logging my information on paper notes, coordinating the tour dates, venues and choirs. And when I made contact with a choir that committed to doing the shows, I would snail mail packages with cassette tapes of the song, and music charts for them to practice their parts. And since the band wanted a consistent look on stage for the choirs every night, I felt it best to carry choir robes on tour. So we organized a large wardrobe case with twenty white choir robes that would be my corner of the traveling circus.

The tour started around March of 1985. I was put on the crew bus with the working crew because I needed to be at the venues much earlier than the band. Every day, in the afternoon, my choir "du jour" would arrive at the backstage area. My job was to ensure they cleared security and received their credentials. Then I would escort them into a specially designated backstage area at the venue. We would rehearse the song, with me blasting my little cassette deck with the tape of the song. Then we would rehearse their staging: how they would walk on stage, where they would stand, how they would move, and how they would walk off. I was labeled the choir "wrangler" by the crew, which might be taken derogatorily today. But the truth be told, the choir was a significant highlight of the show every night. And they and that magic moment needed to be handled with tender, loving care. If nothing else, I understood the egos and hearts of these singers and what the opportunity meant to them.

It was risky business having unknown and unprofessional choirs come into the picture every night. We never knew how good the singers would be from night to night, state to state, country to country. Some were very good church or university choirs that were well-trained and semi-professional. But on average, they were inexperienced, somewhat mediocre singers. Remember, Foreigner was a loud rock band. So there was a lot of volume on stage to contend with in arena-sized venues. And mixing open mics with large groups of people on a live stage is difficult. Therefore, as an insurance backup, the keyboard player Bob Mayo had samples of the original choir from the record that he could trigger during the song. Bob had an Emulator, which was a popular keyboard at the time. It was an 8-bit floppy disk-based keyboard workstation that was a big part of the 80s sound. Depending on how good or not good the choir was, the front-of-house engineer, Mike Renault, would mix in more or less of the sampled vocals that Bob would trigger. I don't think the choirs or the audiences ever knew. But we all knew. Nevertheless, it sounded amazing and conjured the goosebumps, emotional response from the audience that the song inspired. Everyone was thrilled every night when an average of twenty choir members, and sometimes up to two hundred, like at Madison Square Garden, in their flowing white choir robes, would float onto the stage and sing their hearts out. It was a real feel-good, sing-along moment. And as my little reward for my hard work, I would sing a few Jennifer Holiday fills. In my heart, I wanted to be singing more. But it was enough, then, to be instrumental in helping to make that song sparkle for 120 shows or so.

In looking back at how successful a job I did, I wish I had asked for more money. Ha! But I was young and dumb. And honestly, I didn't have a sense of what the job was worth.

Behind the scenes, and it being the 1980s, there were a lot of drugs on that tour. A lot. People were raving on cocaine. It was everywhere. And I think everyone, and I mean everyone, was doing it, including me. And what goes up must come down. Consequently, heavy drinking was the other end of the see-saw of that wound-up madness. Some people also smoked pot to come down, or popped pills: Quaaludes, Valium, Percocet, whatever you could get your hands on was the only way to sleep if you were tanked up on coke. It was a roller coaster of physical abuse, which sometimes led to moody, exhausted mental states, and people not getting along. I think Mick and Lou had their share of head-butting challenges in those days. And I know some guys on the crew had their moments as well.

Being single and riding the tour bus with a crew of young men, I also had a few debauched flings with a guy or two. We were young and wild. I don't regret that. However, in reminiscing, it was the 80s, with AIDS looming in our midst. It was a sexually scary time. But I think many of us heterosexuals were in denial as to whether or not we might get infected. There was a naive sense that it was isolated to the gay community, which was downright ignorant. I'm so relieved that I survived that period disease-free and pretty unscathed. Sadly, there were many people I knew from those days who died young due to the ravages of drug and alcohol abuse, AIDS, cancer, or just the wear and tear of hard living.

The most significant and challenging moment for me on that tour was getting a phone call in the middle of the night in my hotel room in Edinburgh, Canada. I actually don't remember who called me. It might have been my younger sister. But the voice on the other end was informing me that my father had died of heart failure. He was 66 years old.

I was able to go home for a couple of days for my father's funeral, which was a surreal blur. Luckily, because I had well advanced the choirs for the tour, someone on the production crew was able to cover a few shows for me. But I turned right around and jumped back on the tour bus, kind of numb to it all.

I don't think I really processed my father's death until many years later, when I was off the road and in therapy. The microcosm of road life can keep one insulated and separated from real-life experiences and emotional life, because it's a kind of fantasy existence. It's why many people who live that life end up with personal and relationship challenges.

The Agent Provocateur Tour was a small tornado that traversed swaths of North America, Europe, Japan, and even Israel. I shepherded a parade of singers from every country, culture, language, and level of skill, with each one making an indelible impact on the show in that magical moment when the audience would hear the downbeat of the song's introduction, and the earworm effect of the chorus. It's an enduring memory.

Strangely, in recent years, I've realized that that song poetically symbolized what I desired from my relationship with my father all my life. And how it punctuated the impact of his death on me at that time in my twenties.

Ultimately, isn't that the age-old quest for us all?

To love and be loved.

Lou Gramm, Mick Jones & me behind Mick- Farm Aid 1985

Mick Jones & Me- Poughkeepsie, NY 2017

Seven the Hard Way Tour - Pat Benatar

"The dice of Zeus always fall luckily" – Sophocles

After a bit of a rest following the end of the Agent Provocateur Tour, the beginning of 1986 brought an unexpected call from Peyton Wilson, who was the production manager for the Jackson Victory Tour a few years back. He was now the tour manager for Pat Benatar. Patti had decided to add a couple of female background vocalists for her upcoming tour. As her records always had great background vocals, I guess she wanted to add that icing on the cake value to the show.

    I don't remember exactly where my home base was at that time, since I had been bouncing around back and forth from NYC to LA. But because my dear friends Marcene and Danny always offered me a place to stay, I went to the audition in Los Angeles. Luckily, the audition wasn't a big cattle call with a line of singers auditioning. It was more private and low-key compared to most big tours. I remember the full band being there, with me and another woman singing. A cute blonde woman named Marcy Gensic and I were chosen to do the tour. I think it helped that Peyton knew me prior, and he put in a good word for me. That, and maybe being able to hit those high notes on 'Love Is a Battlefield', was definitely a plus. As my husband likes to say, "Show 'em your tits and hit those high notes, baby." He's a funny guy, even if that remark is a little sexist now.

    Seven the Hard Way wasn't a very long tour, maybe six months if that. I think it was a transitional time for Patti and Neil since they had just had their first child, Haley. I remember them telling stories about the difficulties they experienced conceiving her. So they were so happy having little Haley in their lives and being new parents. Haley and her nanny traveled on tour with us. I remember Haley taking some of her first steps on our private tour plane, and it being a celebratory moment. So much of Patti and Neil's attention was directed toward the baby and her care. Perhaps more than toward the tour itself.

Honestly, I think Patti and Neil would have been happy with just staying home with their new little angel, rather than being on the road. But contractual obligations with the record label forced them to release the record and do the tour. I believe there was a bit of conflict with the record label for them, which I don't know much more about. However, in an interview I found on the Ultimate Classic Rock website, Pat is quoted. "No one had any sympathy that your life was totally changed. No one looked at you as a human being, no one looked at you as a woman, no one looked at you as a person. And it was just horrendous," she recalled. "They didn't care, it was just like, 'Okay, great, you had the baby, that's nice, can we just get on with it' - that kind of thing. And they wanted the record immediately. We had nothing done. I was not in the frame of mind to write songs. I was not in the frame of mind to make a record."

Even with that situation brewing in the background, Patti and Neil never let their upset show on stage or off. They were both so solid musically and in their relationship, as they are now. They upheld a cheerful, professional, and kind persona, with me and with everyone. I never had a bad moment with them. In fact, our friendship continued for a while after that tour, with invitations to parties at their house and other gatherings. I'm probably the one who let things slip once I went out with other tours, and ventured off into my own life.

Unfortunately, the Seven the Hard Way Tour was not a big selling tour. Nor did the record do as well as I think everyone had hoped. Even though there are a few memorable singles like 'Sex as a Weapon' and 'La Bel Age', in the overall scheme of her career, it only went gold and had a quick fall. In her memoir, Between a Heart and a Rock Place, Pat said, "Out of all the albums, Seven the Hard Way cost the most to make and sold the least." The album sold approximately 600,000 US copies. Clearly, she wasn't happy with the situation, or the outcome, though many artists today would be thrilled to have that kind of success.

Aside from the great honor and fun of singing with Pat Benatar, one of my fondest memories was striking up a friendship with Patti's personal assistant. Dougal Caron was married to Michael Caron at the time, and since Michael was on the tour as the stage manager, they brought Dougal out to be an assistant. Dougal and I became thick as thieves. We used to hang out after the shows and steal the champagne from Patti's dressing room because she wasn't drinking it. And it was still the 80s remember, so there was a lot of drugs and alcohol being consumed in the "shadows of the night", out of view of the bosses. Though I'm sure they knew we were carrying on like idiots, Pat and Neil never said anything. They just weren't big partiers, especially with a new baby. But Dougal and I, and the guys on the crew, certainly made up for them and then some. Oddly, Marcy didn't hang out with us at all. She kept to herself, from what I recall, so sadly I never got to know her very well. Maybe she felt intimidated by my friendship with Dougal, I don't know.

To this day, Dougal and I talk about how we tore it up on that tour. It was probably a lifesaver that it wasn't a long run, because we probably would have crashed and burned at some point. But it was a lot of fun! And what an honor to have sung with one of the greatest female rock 'n' roll singers ever. Between Patti and Ann Wilson, there are only a few women that I believe have vocally delivered that full-throttle, edgy, powerful rock sound, equivalent to men like Robert Plant, Lou Gramm, or Steve Perry. Freddie Mercury was in a class of his own.

As the popular style and sound of music has evolved significantly today, so too has the vocal vocabulary and sonority of singers. Not to say there aren't great singers out there now. There are a plethora of them. But what seems predominantly thought of as great singing today is either vocalists with heavily melismatic pop and R&B riffing, or whispery thin, seductive vocalism that to me sometimes sounds like people are doing heroin. Of course, that sound can be beautifully intimate. But if that's all a singer can do, it seems limited. Anyway, it's quite a different musical sensibility from back in the day. For the most part, it's shifted away from the approach of someone like a Pat Benatar, and singers like her from that era. Also, I think the development of modern recording technology and auto-tuning has had a big influence on that.

Dougal and I lost touch for a while, each of us living our lives in very different ways. But as life goes in circles, we've reconnected in recent years. Along with Marcene, whom I never really lost touch with, the three of us remain good friends and try to see each other in person at least once a year. It's so gratifying to share our long histories together with many commonalities, music, culture, and experiences. The older I get, the more I appreciate the gift of lasting friendships. Marcene, Dougal, and I still carry on like young girls with a lot of laughs and love. Just without the cocaine craziness.

Warming up backstage: Marcy, Me & Pat Benatar 1986

Dougal, Me & Marcene-Santa Barbara, CA 2022

Moody's Mood - George Benson

"The wise musicians are those who play what they can master"
– Duke Ellington

Early in 1987, I was back living in LA with my friends Marcene and Danny O'Bryen in their house in the San Fernando Valley. Somehow, I got a call from Dennis Turner, who was George Benson's manager at the time, and instrumental in his career development in those years. He also managed Kenny G, who was hot back then as well.

Dennis told me that Vickie Randall, who had been doing the gig for years, was leaving to work with the Tonight Show band. They needed to replace her. The catch was that she was not only the background vocalist, but the percussionist too. While he described the position to me, I remember thinking to myself: "Well, I have good rhythm and I can groove, so how hard could it be?" I said ok, I'd love to do the gig. Ha! Whether it was that naive optimism or delirium, I figured I would get it together somehow.

Luckily, George's organization owned a set of congas and timbales, as well as some small percussion toys. So I didn't need to spend money to get a rig together. I just needed to figure out how to get some basic percussion skills together and learn the material. I had two weeks to get my hands in shape and learn the songs before the start of the European leg of the tour.

Since I had never played congas before, I wanted to take some lessons to get me going with some basic techniques and principles on how and where to place my parts. So I called Mike Fischer, who was a well-known percussionist and studio musician in LA. I asked him if he would help whip me into shape for the gig. He probably doesn't even remember, but his instruction was invaluable. I was able to get a foundation of skills together that got me through. Thank God I have a good sense of rhythm, and I was able to basically fake it. I never heard a bad word from George or anyone else in the band. They were all welcoming and supportive, knowing that percussion wasn't my main instrument. I guess I pulled it off.

The spring and summer of 1987 was a great time, touring with George in Europe. All the big jazz festivals and concert halls were buzzing, like Montreux Jazz, Nice Jazz, The North Sea Jazz Festival in The Hague and so on. We played in places like Umbria in Italy, the casino in Monte Carlo, bull rings in Spain, and places that cater to softer and more sophisticated music. It was a string of shows in a different echelon of places compared to what I had experienced with Foreigner and would see later down the road with Floyd. Many of these places were elegant and old-world, and the promoters and audiences were the same.

I have lovely memories of Claude Nobs, the originator of the Montreux Jazz Festival. He was a worldly, stylish man—bigger than life. He was funny and a wonderful host to all the musicians who played the festival. He loved music and loved hanging out with musicians. Sadly, I understand Claude died after a skiing accident in 2013.

Working with George Benson was working with a true master. Even though he had shifted his career from a serious, straight-ahead jazz guitarist to a more commercially viable singing guitar player, there was no mistaking his virtuosic abilities as a musician. Listening to him every night on that tour, I marveled at his abilities, even within the context of some of his more commercial songs like 'On Broadway'. I'm guessing that audiences often had no idea of the deeply sophisticated and complex ideas he would nonchalantly blaze into during a guitar solo. Or how gorgeously he would sing the Nat King Cole material with a prowess equal to Nat himself. Or the vocal finesse he would display, just like some of those classic 1940s crooners. He was magnificent.

To top it off, George was a gentleman and an elegant dresser. His roots were in the era when musicians wore suits on stage. And he carried himself with a noble confidence, long before the show Bridgerton was even a twinkle of a concept in Shonda Rhimes' head. To me, George was and is musical royalty. Being a very handsome man to begin with, George had a charm and suave way about him that was delightfully old school. He was elegant and loved drinking champagne. I never saw George not smiling or in a bad way. I'm sure he had his moments, but I never saw them. In my short run with him, he was always warm and delightful with me.

One of the most memorable times I had performing with George was playing the Nice Jazz Festival. We played right before Miles Davis on the bill. The vibe was electric. Europeans are such an appreciative audience of jazz music.

After the show, we all went back to the hotel located on the strip of the Côte d'Azur, where it was buzzing with the lusty atmosphere of summer. A bunch of us went down to the hotel bar. It was packed and bustling with musicians who were also staying in the hotel or nearby. I strutted through the hotel lobby, headed for the bar, with Stanley Banks, the bass player. George was there too. I squeezed through the crowd and wiggled up to the bar to order a drink. The next thing I knew, Stanley was behind me, tapping me on the shoulder, announcing that Miles Davis had asked about me and wanted to meet me. According to Stanley, Miles asked "Who's dat bitch?" What? Me? I was stunned. Stanley said, "I think you should go check it out." Really? What did Miles want with me? I was scared and excited all at once. Then a guy named Gordon, who was Miles' personal valet, approached me to take me up to Miles' suite. Off I went.

Standing at the entrance of Miles Davis' hotel suite, my heart was pounding with worry that I had gotten myself into a bad situation. When the door swung open, Miles welcomed me with that famous sandy rasp of a voice of his. As I walked into the main living room of his suite, I realized Gordon had disappeared and closed the door behind me. There were sheets of 8"x 10" art paper strewn all around the living room sofa and table. They were sketches of Miles' artwork. There was a room service cart already set up with a bottle of champagne in a silver bucket with two crystal fluted glasses. He asked if I wanted a glass of champagne. I sheepishly accepted.

With our drinks in hand, he then led me to a beautiful balcony overlooking the Promenade des Anglais and the Mediterranean Sea across from the hotel. It was a beautiful, sultry night. Our conversation was easy and fluid. We spoke about life, music, art, and a myriad of other topics as we sipped champagne and enjoyed the passing of the evening.

Miles was a complete gentleman with me that night. He never made a physical advance, or even hinted at anything sexual or inappropriate. I honestly think he just wanted company, away from the crowds, without any agenda or pressure of being anything other than himself. It was most likely a rare moment for him, and certainly a magical occasion for me. There I was, sitting with a legendary figure in jazz music history, sipping champagne, overlooking the Mediterranean Sea like two old friends. It was extraordinary and precious. A rare moment in time, for my memory alone. My only regret about that night is that I didn't ask for a little piece of his artwork as a keepsake.

George Benson's Band Summer 1987
L-R Barnaby Finch (piano), (B)Steve Tavlioni (sax), (F) Michael O'Neil (gtr), Walt Fowler (trp), George Benson, Me, Stanley Banks (bass), (B-R) David Garfield (keys), (MR) Albert Wing (sax), Bubba Bryant (drm) (FR) unknown

The Delicate Sound of Thunder Tour

"There's no sensation to compare with this, suspended animation, a state of bliss" - David Gilmour

In mid-summer 1987, my European run with George Benson ended, and I landed back in LA with Marcene and Danny. I was renting a room in their house at the time, because with being single and on the road a lot, it didn't make sense to have an apartment. When I got home, I thought I would have some relaxing downtime. But out of the blue, I received a call from Malcolm Craggs, the tour manager for Pink Floyd. What? How? They had gotten my name and number from Buford Jones, who was the front-of-house mix engineer for the Pat Benatar tour I did the year before. I was floored!

As I tell my students now, you just never know where your next opportunity will come from. Being professional, doing a good job, trying to be a nice person, and networking are all important parts of building and sustaining a career. I realize more networking is done on social media nowadays, but ultimately, I still think that in-person interactions and relationships are much more impactful. But I digress.

I was instructed to meet David Gilmour at the Village Recording Studio in West LA, where he was working with Bob Ezrin finishing up the Momentary Lapse of Reason album. I was in a daze. It was a typically hot, sweltering summer day in LA. I met with David in the central lounge of that studio building. After our introductory formalities, we moved into a very friendly, easy conversation. I was in disbelief and secretly wondering when I was going to wake from my dream. He was the consummate English gentleman and lovely with me. I can't imagine him being any other way, frankly. I don't know what Buford told David, but I never had to sing for him. No song and dance. No casting couch. In fact, there was very little conversation about music. After spending what seemed like a flash of an instant together, he just said, "So do you want to go on tour?" And that was that.

As is fairly well known to Floyd fans, the full rehearsals for the tour began in August 1987, a month before the live shows were scheduled to start. The production was obscured in an Air Canada airplane hanger on the outskirts of Toronto. It was strategically hidden away from the general public in the most acoustically unusual place for loud electric music. But for the sake of the rehearsals for that huge stage production, with massive dangling lights overhead, lasers, a flying bed, a gigantic pig, projectiles coming out of the stage, pyro, and a colossal film screen behind us, it was a necessary container to trial-run a monstrosity of a show. We were set to play only stadiums and arenas that could contain a show of this proportion. It was a mechanical behemoth on wheels with endless moving parts.

When I arrived in Toronto, I was as nervous as a newborn lamb. Unsteady and unsure of myself. I had never been a singer for a band quite that big. Though with the Jackson Victory Tour, Pat Benatar and Foreigner behind me, I was at least familiar with the size and scope of a show at that level. That's not the part that scared me. Previously, it seemed I was walking behind the elephant somehow. But now I had to get on top of this big animal and ride it. It's the place I'd always dreamed I'd get to. And suddenly, there I was. I knew I had to step up my game vocally and otherwise. For one thing, physically, the background singers were set up right in the frontline of the stage, so there was no hiding. And the weight of the name of the band attracted a lot of attention. Moreover, it was the first Floyd tour without Roger Waters. It was the first time David, Nick, and Rick were the controlling members of the band. And it was the first tour since The Wall in the early 1980s. So it was important to them that this tour was successful.

Like with any relationship, beginnings are always sweet. Everyone is on their best behavior, just getting to know each other. The guys were great. Scott Page and I immediately connected, being the only Americans in the band other than Jon Carin. Also, because of Scott's outgoing, positive personality, it was easy to befriend him. Jon Carin, on the other hand, seemed like he wanted to disassociate from being American. It seemed to me that he rather fancied himself an Anglophile, donning a slightly fake British accent with a bit of a chip on his shoulder. That said, he was and still is massively talented, and I never had a bad moment with him. Truthfully, he just came across as self-absorbed and distant. But to be fair, he was young too, and figuring out the lay of the land like we all were.

Gary Wallis, on the other hand, was and still is a crazy, pisser of a character. He was a badass drummer/percussionist even then, hilariously funny, and a heavy partier. These days, he's the musical director and drummer for Tom Jones, a respected position he's had for thirty years. I'm happy to say we're still in touch.

Guy Pratt, who was a young lion of a bass player, also had that wicked British wit. He, too, was a pretty heavy partier who took it beyond the edge. I understand he had some serious issues with his drugging and drinking through the years, but has since recovered a healthy equilibrium.

Mind you, everyone back in the day was taking it out with partying. It was part of the culture. Most of us were in our twenties, fit, and riding high with the frenzy of the end of the 1980s party lifestyle that was a carryover from the disco days of the late 1970s. Cocaine and alcohol-fueled social activities across social status lines infiltrated everywhere, from the music industry, restaurant culture, and club culture, to Wall Street and middle-class weekend warriors. It felt to me that the whole world was partying in the 1980s.

Looking back, the world was on fire then with the ideals of materialism, consumerism, and money. It was the emergence of the yuppie generation, cable TV networks like CNN, and MTV. It was a rapidly changing socio-political terrain. That was the same period that brought Reagan-omics and AIDS, which was raging in the background of our young heterosexual lives. Maybe that's why so many of us wanted to check-out with drugs and alcohol. It felt like a bewildering and dangerous time, much like now. It was the ramp-up slope to everything changing with the World Wide Web and the Dot-com boom soon approaching. Life would never be the same.

Tim Renwick was the secondary guitar player to Gilmour. I remember him as being such a lovable soul. He was a sweetheart and gentleman with me. Sure, he liked his cigarettes and booze too. But I don't remember him being so out of hand, like some of us. Or he had that uncanny English ability to wear it well. Also, he was a little bit older and perhaps wiser. He was already experienced as a successful studio musician and toured with some other substantial groups on the road prior to Floyd. Either that, or I was oblivious to what was really going on for him. At that time, he had a relationship with the manager's assistant Jane Sen on the tour. She was a lovely person and they were sweet together. They gracefully tried to keep their involvement discreet, but we all knew they were an item. Road relationships are a very tricky business for anyone. Jane and Tim stayed together for some time after the tour. Later, Jane, whom I recently spoke with, ended up marrying manager Tony Smith and doing great. I'm so happy for her.

David, Nick, and Rick, to me, were the bosses. In my mind, there was a professional line they had to uphold, and one that I didn't dare cross with them. Whether it was my young fear of power, or just the way I was brought up, I tried to stay out of their way and in my place. They didn't party as much as the sidemen and singers. That said, Dave and Rick definitely had their moments of hanging out, much more than Nick. I recall that Rick always had a cigarette in his hand, which sadly contributed to his demise in the end. To me, he was the sweetest of them all.

Aside from a general overlying sense of debauchery that occurred on that tour, there are a few particular party moments that stand out in my mind. Dave and a few of the guys dropped acid a few times during some shows. I don't know how they did it. Honestly, I didn't even know until after the fact. I remember another scene in a downtown NYC restaurant where after a group dinner, someone laid out lines of cocaine on top of the table in the middle of the restaurant, and we were snorting them right there in public. It was the raging eighties after all. Then there is a distinct vision I retain of everyone blitzed on ecstasy one night in a night club in Australia on a night off. I must admit that it was insanely fun at the time. Though I shudder now, when I think about how risky and stupid some of that behavior was. Miraculously, I and most everyone survived that madness, and always kept it together when it came to doing the show. Fast forward to now, I would never have imagined I would be taking ecstasy thirty-five years later as a therapeutic aide.

Nick, to me, was the straightest of the bunch. He rarely hung out. He seemed much more settled down with his girlfriend, Nettie, who he later married. Perhaps Nick felt a responsibility to uphold his professional persona and remain in charge. I'm not sure. Or he had his fill of partying before. I never got to speak with him in-depth very much. He wasn't much of a talker to me. Nevertheless, not only did Dave, Nick, and Rick have to play and sing well every night, but like any professional in their position, they had to do press, promo, and deal with the legalities of the day-to-day business of the tour. Even with Steve O'Rourke at the management helm then, they stayed intimately involved.

In 1987, as many people know, Pink Floyd was entwined in a pretty nasty lawsuit. Roger Waters had left the band and wanted to retain ownership of the name and brand. Dave, Nick, and Rick made their own claim. It's not my place to go into that, but the tension and drama were palpable. We were all aware of what was going on behind the scenes with that situation. Clearly, it all worked out for Dave, Nick, and Rick in the settling of that lawsuit. They retained ownership of the Pink Floyd name and brand, and the Delicate Sound of Thunder Tour and those following were hugely successful. Roger, with his formidable identity and brilliance, consequently had his own successes with his music later on.

Truthfully, I always felt a bit shy around David, Nick, and Rick back then. Yet they were so warm and generous with all of us professionally. There was very little ego flexing, I felt, with any of them, while they certainly could have done so. They were, after all, rock stars. But they all treated everyone in the band with professional respect and let us do our thing. It was truly about the music and the vibe for them.

When you're living with people for a year on a tour like that, there is an intimacy you experience by the sheer nature of the work and lifestyle. You're living and traveling together in a sheltered cocoon of existence, protected by a shield of security guards, and under the umbrella of celebrity. It's an exclusive microcosm bubble of a lifestyle experienced by few.

In keeping with a high level of professionalism, the band and management of Pink Floyd made sure we were all well taken care of. We always stayed in the best hotels like the Ritz Carltons or Four Seasons, which at the time were top notch. We traveled by private jet whenever possible. I even remember Learjets taking us to some shows in Europe. Otherwise, they booked business or first-class tickets for our travel. The backstage catering and after show hospitality set ups were extravagant. The champagne flowed every night, along with anything else you'd want to imbibe. Platters of sushi decorated long tables of various delectable delights as standard fare. The atmosphere was lavish and rich. No expense was spared to make us all feel like rock stars. It was a rock n'roll dream in living color that I look back on with awe and gratitude.

In retrospect, I pinch myself when I remember that I truly lived through that incredibly magical time, despite the internal struggles I had to juggle. It was a rarified experience that so few people get to claim. But I did it. And in a big way. It's a part of my personal and professional history, as well as rock music legend. No one and nothing can take that away from me.

Delicate Sound of Thunder band photo 1987

(left to right)
Jon Carin, Scott Page, David Gilmour, Me, Nick Mason, Rich Wright,
Rachel Fury, Gary Wallis, Tim Renwick, Guy Pratt
Photo by Dimo Safari
With permission from Sony Records

Learning To Fly
The Delicate Sound of Thunder Tour

"You are not meant for crawling, so don't. You have wings. Learn to use them and fly" - Rumi

At the start of the tour, there were only Rachel Fury and me as the background vocalists. It was just the two of us all through the rehearsals in Toronto, all the way until the dates in Atlanta and the first filming event. I'm not sure why. Perhaps Dave and the management thought they could save money by getting away with just two singers, but it would later change, for several reasons.

It was a rough start from the very beginning with Rachel. She was cold and competitive with me. She would barely speak to me unless something really needed to be said. Yet, when she turned around to speak with Dave or any of the guys in the band, she transformed into a charming coquette. Her passive-aggressive way toward me really pushed my buttons. It activated my feelings of insecurity and doubt. I honestly never understood why she was that way with me. Was I not good enough for her? Pretty enough? Maybe I was too tall? Maybe it was because I was Japanese and weird-looking to her. My shadow side kicked in hard back then. At the time, I didn't understand the Jungian concept of the shadow side, but I clearly remember how I felt.

I had to fight as diligently as possible not to let my inner emotional turmoil show on the surface. I didn't want it to affect my singing or my sense of professionalism in the situation. I tried not to let it affect my attitude and my enjoyment of the experience. But it was secretly gnawing at me and it was exhausting. I tried my best to camouflage my discomfort. It was such a dichotomy to the glorious and glistening exterior of my surrounding reality.

Rachel had gotten the gig through her relationship with James Guthrie, a longtime recording engineer for Floyd. She was a good, strong alto with an edgy upper belt. I always thought it was a nice juxtaposition to my voice. I'm a strong, clean soprano with a piercing upper mix and a little whistle tone thrown in. I think we could have made it work well with just the two of us musically. But truthfully, with the enormous amount of sound forged by all the musicians and amps on the stage, there was a lot of competition for sonic space. And with a third harmony, it would definitely prove to be a better overall blend. Nevertheless, the bigger issue was that Rachel and I simply weren't clicking.

In the beginning, I tried many times to confront her nicely and ask her what was wrong. But she wasn't having it. She simply didn't make an effort to try and be friends. It was a dreadful setup in the middle of an ideal professional situation. I didn't know how we would survive a year of touring together like that. Frankly, in looking back, she was a bitch to me.

None of us are invisible in life, no matter how we try. And the band and management saw what was going on between us girls. I knew that if things didn't change, one of us might get fired. I remember talking to Steve O'Rourke one night about the situation with Rachel. In addition, I had heard that Rachel was making more money than me, which wasn't fair. So I needed to engage his help to set things straight.

Steve was a tall, sturdy build of a man, with bottle-thick glasses that sat above his no-nonsense square jaw. He had a bit of a frightening presence to me, which, for a manager, is a good thing. Though it was a bit distressing to have to speak with him, he also had a softer side, especially if you were a woman. A much younger woman at that. One night after one of the early shows in September, everyone was hanging out, drinking, and carrying on as usual. It was such an exciting time, with the shows selling out and the tour launching off to a meteoric start. I apprehensively chatted up Steve to discuss my dilemma, and he listened. Our conversation progressed to ending up later that night in my hotel room. Needless to say, one thing led to another. I got my raise.

Remember, it was long before the #MeToo movement, and social politics for women were quite different back then. So after that night of commiserating with Steve, the prescription to solve the problem with Rachel would soon be revealed.

The band was planning to do various recordings and filming of upcoming shows throughout the tour. First up would be in Atlanta, scheduled for November 3rd-5th, 1987. It was at the Omni Coliseum, which was at the time home to the Atlanta Hawks basketball team. It seated 16,000 plus people. It's sadly since been demolished.

In order to spice things up for the film, the film producer was asked to bring in a few more "girls", to act as additional background singers for the shoot. It was presented as a one-time deal, visually dressing up the stage for just those shows. Cut to the introduction of Durga McBroom, Lorelei McBroom, and Roberta Freeman. For anyone who's seen those clips from the Atlanta shows, in some of the shots you can see Durga, me, and Roberta on stage right. And Rachel and Lorelei are on stage left. Another night it was switched up. At the end of the run of those shows, Steve offered a position to Lorelei initially. She was committed to a record deal at the time, so Durga jumped in. Durga being a low alto, was the perfect musical fit. And she was placed right smack dab in the middle of the drama between Rachel and me. With Durga's outspoken personality, she wasn't having any bullshit. In fact, she was instructed by Steve O'Rourke to make sure things chilled out in the vocal section. And they did.

Durga, with her strong presence, was just the block of energy we needed to stomp out the silent sparks between Rachel and me. Like two magnets of similar poles, I suspect that the repelling nature of our personalities was caused by the fact that Rachel was just as insecure as I was. But she had a much tougher shield of a persona. Many times, those that seem the toughest are secretly the most insecure.

With the addition of Durga, for the rest of the tour our little corner of the stage got on much better. The rough edges were smoothed out. And we ended up having a really good time, for the most part. How could we not have fun singing in front of thousands of adoring Pink Floyd fans in stadiums and arenas worldwide on a first-class tour like that? I believe at some point, we all realized the glorious gem we had in our hands.

After the Delicate Sound of Thunder Tour, Rachel strangely disappeared. To my knowledge, she vanished from the music industry. There are various and puzzling rumors regarding her absence from the limelight and social media. It's a mystery that many adoring fans and I would love to know the answer to.

Wherever she is now, I hope she's happy. It would have been nice to speak with her again as mature adults and make peace with those awkward moments from our youth. I want to think that now, we could both laugh about the stupidity of the past and find a place of mutual understanding and forgiveness.

It's said that it's never good to go to bed angry. On a grander scale, I don't want to go to my grave carrying regrets from the past.

Rachel and me during rehearsals in Toronto 1987

Me , Durga & Rachel

A Momentary Lapse in Reason

"Good judgment comes from experience, and a lot of that comes from bad judgment" - Will Rogers

On the first day of setup for the filming in Atlanta, the arena was a beehive of activity with crew, cameras, extra lights, and whatever else needed to be constructed to make all that film magic happen. It's incredible to witness when crews magically throw together what I think of as living art projects. The power of cooperation and artistry that goes into birthing these creative acts is nothing short of a miracle.

Stepping out on stage for a soundcheck and some run-throughs for the cameras and lights, I immediately noticed one of the guys who seemed to be directing other people and seemed to have some crucial creative role. He was dark, macho, and kind of attractively mysterious to me. He smiled at me from the floor, and some magnetic pull from the universe drew me in. Little did I know that it would be a nefarious trick of fate to get involved with this man. Unbeknownst to me, a communion with him would be the biggest heart-wrenching train wreck, break-me-at-the-knees episode. Meeting this person and the trials and tribulations that would ensue would initiate an incomprehensibly arduous chapter that would take me years to recover from. But it needed to happen. To not incriminate myself or anyone else, and for the sake of my story, let's call him Bruno.

Bruno was a very talented cinematographer. At that point, he had been very successful in shooting commercials and music videos, which were big business then. Remember, MTV was still a fairly young cable channel and a hot commodity at that time. Music videos were a growing marketing tool for performing artists. And they offered great career opportunities for the creative people who made visual voodoo. It was an electrifying scene.

On the outside, Bruno was an intriguing individual. Not because he was so handsome, but because he was creative and successful in a happening scene. And just to clear the air here, I am not talking about Marc Reshovsky or Wayne Isham, who are credited with shooting the Delicate Sound of Thunder film. Bruno didn't end up with credits on the final cut, as far as I can tell. I'm not sure about the details of that.

Our relationship started out hot and heavy. A downpour of romantic attention and desperate hotel phone calls. I started seeing him at first on a tour break. Then he visited me on tour a few times, which, in retrospect, was a mistake. From the beginning, Bruno was very generous. He showered me with beautiful jeweled trinkets and girlie gifts every time I would see him. No one had ever done that with me before. He took me to posh restaurants. He spent money on extravagant jaunts and alluring experiences—things I never had growing up as a middle-class girl from a dysfunctional family in New Jersey.

So along came Bruno, seducing me with lavish adornments: diamond bracelets, lingerie, and exotic trips. I was lulled into a stupor. His tactics induced a kind of blindness that averted my heart away from the red flags flapping in the wind right in front of my face. Because truthfully, buried under the fantastic facade he presented lived an insecure, jealous, controlling nature that oversexualized women, and a deep-seated anger that would soon be revealed and acted out on me once I was trapped in his web. And because of my emotionally damaged heart, it was the perfect setup for me to reengage with my subconscious familial demons.

It's said in psychology that we attract people into our lives who help us work out our issues and grow. Well, that couldn't be truer in this situation. Bruno turned out to be the Pluto to my Venus. The sting of Scorpio to my fragile Libra heart. He mirrored all the unconscious darkness that I hid and ran away from. He represented my father's dysfunction and my mother's dysfunction rolled up in one. It was the perfect framework for me to play out the mirroring of a relationship I learned from my parents. It was toxic. Eventually, he brilliantly figured out all my insecurities and self-doubt to the point that he knew how to control me, tear me down, and render me helpless. Of course, there are always silent agreements in relationships. So I unconsciously allowed him to destroy me and played the role of the victim like my mother. In hindsight, it's what needed to happen to wake me up.

When I got off the road with Floyd at the end of 1988, I went back to Los Angeles to live with Bruno. I felt lost after coming off a very long tour and a string of work over several years. I missed everyone on the tour, but I didn't know what the next step would be for my career. My weakened and exhausted state of mind turned into dependency on him. And that dependency turned into me not having control over myself. He became more and more emotionally abusive. And that abuse slowly escalated into the physical. Bruises and fractured bones were not just dramatic descriptions. They became the secret theater of the relationship, behind closed doors. The abuser and the abused were floundering in the dark. Not pretty.

Because of the imprinting from my family history, I kept thinking it was somehow my fault. And in retrospect, that was the pattern of thinking that became a theme in my life with a number of relationships in the past. I know now it's typical of the children of alcoholics and broken family structures to blame themselves. And it's very typical of victims of abuse. With that comes the development of all kinds of coping mechanisms and behaviors, good and bad, in adulthood in order to mitigate those feelings. You do what it takes to survive.

Mix that up with my Japanese heritage and being a woman, and it's a lethal combination. I tried to hide it from the world and put on a brave face. Just like in my childhood, I masqueraded to the world that life was good while harboring a lot of shame and sadness. It was textbook. Needless to say, I didn't consciously see it at the time.

Bruno and I got married with a big, lavish wedding at St Patrick's Cathedral in NYC, and an extravagant reception at the Rainbow Room. It was the ultimate cover-up. We stayed together for about six years. The reason we survived for so long was that he traveled frequently for his work. And I traveled enough so that, in reality, we may have actually lived together just a few years. They were the unhappiest, most onerous years of my life. When I finally hit bottom, the aftermath was a paradigm shattering event.

During that time I was living with him in LA, I turned down the opportunity to go back on the road with Pink Floyd for the Venice show, and consequently missed later tours. I also turned down an offer from the Rolling Stones and a few other bands. That's a regret that still haunts me a bit. Instead, Bruno convinced me to accept an offer to be a lead singer for an LA based band, so I could be home more. I signed a three-year contract that kept me locked up professionally, and with him. More on that later.

Various incidents of physical abuse occurred during the years we were together, though it's needless to go into the gory details. But to give an idea of what sparked those incidents, an example is that if I didn't keep a spotless and tidy house, he would accuse me of being lazy and lame. It would be an excuse for him to yell and degrade me. Also, he would lustfully stare at beautiful women in public and accuse me of being overly sensitive and insecure if I said anything about it. He also had an obsession with pornography and accused me of being a prude because I didn't subscribe to his perversity. These situations and more became triggers for him to act out on me. It sounds dramatic, but unfortunately, as I learned later, these are the kind of situations typical of predatory, abusive people. You never know what will set them off. It's life walking around a ticking time bomb.

I finally left LA and that marriage in 1994. I knew that if I didn't leave, I might end up dead. And I would never be able to get my life back on track and heal my wounds. It was one of the most difficult things I've ever done. But one of the most self-loving and significant maneuvers of my life.

It's strange when I look back on that time. Even though I was in such turmoil in that relationship, leaving it represented a major shift in breaking ties with my family history. I was able to recover myself, and let go of a lot of the pain and shame I carried for so many years. And I shed the victim mentality that influenced me for a long time. It helped me, after a lot of therapy and work on myself, to let go of the anchor tethered to my past that dragged me down and didn't belong to me.

A therapist once told me, "One day I saw a patient of mine and asked how he was doing. The patient said, 'I'm knee-deep in shit, but it's my shit, so I'm doing great'." That was me back then.

When I reminisce about that shattered shell of a person I was then, it's hard to relate to her now. Who was that girl? I know there were parts of me that needed to go through those difficulties—to walk through the fire to be purified. Luckily, now, that person is just a faint shadow of ash absorbed into my memories. When I look back, it feels like another lifetime ago. Truthfully, I'm so grateful for how the challenge of that experience forced me to grow, and guided me to eventually find my true self, and claim the self-love I was missing.

On the Turning Away

"The time is gone, the song is over, thought I'd something more to say" – Pink Floyd

In remembering my time with Pink Floyd, I feel there are no words to encapsulate the impact it made on my life. It was magical. It was life-changing. It was career-affirming. That experience left an indelible mark that brought me so many opportunities both professionally and personally. And the gifts seem to keep coming.

There are unforgettable moments from that time on tour with Floyd that are burned into my memory. Performing on stage facing the Palace of Versailles with hundreds of thousands of people under a full moon was a surreal setting straight out of a movie. Legendary. Playing at the Reichstag in front of the Berlin Wall in 1988, which would ultimately be torn down the following year, and change history, was monumental. Historical. Experiencing the Australian Bicentenary celebration… floating on a majestic old sailboat with bandmates and friends, bobbing in the bay with hundreds of other spectators in Sydney Harbor with a canopy of fireworks blazing overhead the Sydney Opera House is forever etched in my mind. Monumental. Performing in my home state of New Jersey at Giant Stadium, with family and friends witnessing the grandeur, was a heartwarming and proud moment. And my return to Madison Square Garden as a singer with Floyd was a magnificent milestone. These incredible moments, with the band as it was, will never happen again.

Singing with Pink Floyd truly established me as a professional singer on a high, professional level. Particularly with the challenge and opportunity to sing 'Great Gig in the Sky' every night, a vocal highlight in the show, which helped to nurture my vocal abilities to another level. Performing in that big arena rock concert setting gave me a powerful sense of confidence, knowing I could sing with anyone, in almost any musical situation.

As a result of my credential of working with the original Pink Floyd, I've performed with several Pink Floyd tribute bands, of which there are many around the world. There are the two big ones: Brit Floyd and The Australian Pink Floyd. Then there are many smaller outfits in operation. It speaks of the enduring impact of Pink Floyd's music and brand.

In May and August of this year, 2025, I was called to work with Brit Floyd, helping them fill a spot for one of their background singers for a few days. They are led by musical director, guitarist and vocalist Damian Darlington, and bassist and vocalist Ian Catell. I was greatly impressed with the level of musicianship of all the players and singers. Guitarist Edo Scordo, multi-instrumentalist Ryan Saranich, keyboardist Matt Riddle, drummers Randy Cooke and Arran Ahmun are superb. And the beautiful background singers Eva Avila and Genevieve Little were a delight to work with. The production, the sound, the lights, and the stage set were as close to the original Pink Floyd as one could get on a smaller budget scale. The manager, Andy Robbins, and all the crew took great care of me. I venture to say that they are the best Pink Floyd tribute band in the world. I had a fantastic time with them and I made some lovely new friends.

On a different level, there is the band Pinks One in Sicily, with whom I've worked numerous times. And with whom I've established some lasting friendships over the years. Alessandro de Mauro, who is the band leader, guitar player and lead singer, and the principal members of the group - Andrea Zanti (gtr/vox), Seby Aprile (drums), Daniele Scorce (bass), and Gian Luigi Di Gregorio (keys) - have organized an excellent ensemble honoring the Pink Floyd legacy. A few years ago, Scott Page and Gary Wallis joined us on some shows, which was a brilliant bash of a time! The three of us reconnecting, reminiscing about old times, and playing music together again was especially endearing. I've worked with them several times to date, and my relationship with them has blossomed into a warm and endearing friendship.

In northern Italy, there is a band called Wit Matrix. The lovely Claudio Palliati is the leader and bass player, with the other members, Mirko Zanotto (lead vox), Andrea Tadiotto (elec gtr, steel gtr), Nicola Pending (elec gtr), Claudio Tisso (keys), Andrea Basson (drums), Andrea Farina (sax), and their wonderful background vocalists, Serena Pasinato, Marta Melchiori, and Antonia Pia. They are all wonderfully talented and lovely people. They, too, do a phenomenal job of honoring the Floyd catalogue with great musical integrity.

Pink Sound, led by Domenico "Mimmo" Carazita, who I almost did a show with, invited me, along with Durga, to Turin in September 2023. While we were doing a soundcheck for a performance to be a feature of a big air show spotlighting the Italian Air Force's Frecce Tricolori, one of the planes crashed while doing a practice run at a neighboring airstrip. The pilot ejected before the plane hit the ground. Sadly, the downed plane slid violently across the runway in a ball of fire, smashing uncontrollably through the fence and striking a passing car on the road just outside the airport. The car was occupied by a beautiful young family: two adults in the front, and two children in the back seat. Their little girl was killed upon the fiery impact.

Needless to say, the show was appropriately canceled. It was a surreal situation that stunned us all. I'll never forget that day. Nor will anyone else who was there. I still ponder from time to time about the parents of that little girl. What sinister forces of fate could have planned them being the doomed victims of that unfortunate circumstance? Being in precisely in the wrong place at the wrong time. It's a powerful and sad memory locked in my mind.

Lastly, there was a singular show with a Pink Floyd tribute band led by Matias Guiraldes Palma in Chile. He invited Durga, Lorelei, Scott Page and myself to be a part of a grand concert to celebrate the Delicate Sound of Thunder record. It had been thirty-five years since we had done that together. The producers of the show organized us all coming to Chile, paid us, put us up, and covered all the expenses involved. It was a huge undertaking for a relatively small, local conglomerate. The band was a very talented group of musicians, and everyone involved couldn't have been more warm and welcoming. We had a fantastic time!

The show took place in what seemed to me to be a questionable area in Santiago, which I felt a bit uneasy about. I wondered if any local people may have felt the same about coming to a show in that location. It was a very large, industrial-feeling club space that was part of an urban shopping mall in a downtown area, surrounded by what appeared to me to be a dangerous neighborhood. Everyone assured us that it was fine, but not to go out alone. Red flag? Unfortunately, I don't think the concert ticket sales did as well as they had expected. In fact, I think the promoters lost money on the deal, despite being very happy with all of us and the performance. It's a hard pill to swallow when people have such grandiose expectations about shows and they don't deliver the hoped-for results.

These guest appearances with these tribute bands have been a later-in-life benefit from my association with the original Pink Floyd. The fact that the music has such incredible staying power gives it a currency beyond the music business of the day. And its relevance remains potent for people of all ages all over the world. I've even noticed that Pink Floyd embossed T-shirts have become pop culture fashion, along with other rock legends of the past. I often wonder how long that trend will last, but it doesn't seem to be slowing down anytime soon.

Also, it's been such a kick to work again with Durga, Lorelei, Scott and Gary in recent years. It's funny how it feels like not much time has passed since I've seen them, even though it's been over thirty-five years. Both Durga and Lorelei have managed to actualize careers singing with various Floyd groups around the world, and make a living doing so. I have a lot of respect for them, hanging in there and being so industrious. And Scott and Gary have been successful in their own right with various musical projects and business adventures over the years.

In 2023, I toured with Gov't Mule doing a Live Nation production of the Dark Side of the Mule show, honoring the 50th anniversary of the release of The Dark Side of the Moon. It was a familiar somatic rush, singing those songs to enthusiastic audiences around America for a month with an amazing band.

Warren Haynes, who I believe is in the ranks of one of the best rock 'n' roll guitar players ever, held down the Gilmour chair on guitar and vocals. Danny Louis brilliantly honored Rick Wright's world of keyboard textural landscaping in a way Rick would've been proud of. Kevin Scott, a recent welcome addition to Mule, brought a solid, low-end burn to the music with his dazzling touch. And Matt Abts laid the rhythm down, reminiscent of Nick Mason, but with his exclusive flair. Jackie Green on auxiliary guitar, keys and vocals, plus the great Ron Holloway on sax, rounded out the authenticity of the music with an original twist. And on vocals, my friend Sophia Ramos, a great vocalist from NYC, brought her gorgeous grit to blend with my smoother soprano lilt. We made for a great team.

Though the Floyd background vocals have traditionally been three voices, Sofia and I figured out how to make the parts sound full, particularly on 'Great Gig in the Sky'. We each had a section to sing, she singing the opening section, and me singing the end section. In between, we discovered a way to macramé the middle section in harmony that brought the house down every night.

Doing that one-month tour was enough of a delectable taste of road life again to satisfy me for some time. And it was a great reminder of the how and why I don't need that life anymore. It reminded me that I did the right thing by moving on years ago in search of a more fulfilling life for myself. That it was ok for me to not need that particular emblem of existence like I once did. Life and things are forever changing. And to resist those changes is to remain painfully stuck in a definition of oneself that no longer serves you. I certainly had those moments too, of not knowing how or when to let go of what was finished. But I eventually did. Been there, done that. Next!

I've always been and will forever be a restless seeker, pushing to move forward. Doing that tour with Mule was the perfect rerun of an old movie, and a dip in familiar waters. From that tour, I realized that those waters are swampy and stagnant for me now. They no longer satiate me the way they once did. But a once in a while visit to that nostalgic place is a sweet remembrance of what was. My identity no longer needs to spend all my time and energy there. Time is so precious to me now. However, as long as performing work brings me joy, and my body and voice hold out, I'm happy to take it on for ol' time's sake.

As for my relationships with David Gilmour, Nick Mason, and others of the crew, they've pretty much come to an end. On David's recent 2024 tour, I contacted his management simply looking to come and say hello to David and the gang at the Madison Square Garden show. The manager stonewalled me, as if I were a punter off the street. I know he has done the same with Durga and others of us who actually have history with the band. Seemingly, the management and David's wife have built an insular moat of protection around David's world, not to be penetrated by anyone they deem unimportant. David is, after all, the golden goose. And his new handlers are protective of their treasure, which is certainly their prerogative. I respect and understand why.

That said, it hurts a little to have been stripped of the privilege of sharing a friendly visit with someone whom I shared an incredible time with in my professional life. And for whom I have tremendous admiration.

I haven't tried to directly contact Nick. But it would be lovely to see him and his wife again So for now, the memories will have to suffice.

I have to say, I doubt that any of that heavy-handed posturing would be happening if Steve O'Rourke were still alive and managing David. Or if David was still married to Ginger. Just my opinion.

C'est comme ça. La vie continue!

Mom, David Gilmour & me backstage at Giant Stadium 1987

Me and David Gilmour backstage at Madison Square Garden 2016

With Gov't Mule & Jason Bonham's Led Zeppelin Band
Wolftrap Aug 2023
photo by Joshua Hitchens
(Left to Right)
Dorian Heartsong, James Dylan, Sophia Ramos, Danny Louis, Matt Abts, Kevin Scott, Warren Haynes, Jason Bonham, Alex Howland, Jackie Greene, Me, Jimmy Sakurai

With Brit Floyd 2025
Matt Riddle, Genevieve Little, Eva Avila, Edo Scordo, Ian Cattell, Me, Damian Darlington, Ryan Saranich, Randy Cooke

Roots and Realizations – Hiroshima

"Cultural legacies are powerful forces. They have deep roots and long lives" - Malcolm Gladwell

At the end of the Pink Floyd tour, or any tour for that matter, one never knows what your next gig will be. So when I was immediately offered a contract to be a lead singer for the LA-based band named Hiroshima, I grabbed the offer, with a lot of encouragement from my ex. They were already signed to Epic Records with a touring schedule, so it sounded good on paper. Their name too, held powerful symbolism of the post WWII Japanese spirit of surviving the devastating horror of the atomic bombs which destroyed the cities of Hiroshima and Nagasaki. The phoenix rising from the ashes.

The band Hiroshima had been around for a long time. They originally formed in 1974 with their first record release in 1979 on Arista Records. They were unique, and maybe the first Asian American band in the American contemporary music scene. They were classified as a "smooth jazz" or "New Age jazz" styled group, which was a sharp turn away from the gritty rock scene I had just come from.

Other than my immediate family, I had never had any Japanese or Asian friends growing up. And I certainly had never encountered any Asian American musicians in the business back then. It was an intriguing endeavor for me to jump into a situation with people of a similar cultural heritage as mine. It was a kind of return to my roots; my Kunta Kinte moment if you will, that I thought would be enriching.

Right from the get-go, the band had me sign an exclusive contract forbidding me from working with anyone else. On one hand, it felt special. But in hindsight, it should have been a warning sign for me. Never before had I made such a commitment to a single band or a designated gig for a specified period of time. But I signed on to see where it would all lead. Nothing ventured, nothing gained.

Little by little, as my relationship developed with the band and we got into gigging, I began to see that the band's interpersonal dynamics were quite complicated and long-standing. Dan Kuramoto, the band leader, and June, his ex-wife, were the originators and cornerstones of the organization. Although they had been divorced for a while, their relationship still dominated the group's politics and business. Red flag.

June was and still is a gifted koto player and was to me the main element that gave Hiroshima its signature sound. She was a sweetheart to me. But in many ways, she was a strong driving force behind the scenes. Superficially, she presented the persona of a traditional Japanese-American woman. In truth, I suspected the dynamic was different behind closed doors. But in public, it seemed she existed under the dominating force of Dan, not only as his ex, but under his thumb as the band leader. It soon became evident to me that I would be relegated to the same status in the pecking order as the other woman in the band.

Dan and I started to butt heads early on, though subtly at first. I was instructed on how to sing and phrase things, wasn't allowed to participate in writing material for the band, nor did I feel I was given much respect for my musical ideas. Basically, I felt like I was being controlled by a man who hadn't fallen far from that cultural tree. Even though he desperately tried to present himself as a hip, cool American guy, his discriminating demeanor was built into his DNA. Subconsciously, he was probably struggling with his own sense of identity and powerlessness as a person of color in a white man's world, which I can completely understand and feel compassion toward. That said, it wasn't long into my relationship with the band that I felt I had made a big mistake by joining them.

Since I was contracted to a three-year commitment, I had to figure out how to make the best of it. So all I could do was to do my best as a singer and the front person when it was my time to go to bat. As I got established as their front person, I started to get a lot of attention and adulation for my performances. Even journalists gave me rave reviews, like the one from the LA Times for our performance at the Playboy Jazz Festival.

"Blessed with a powerful voice, astonishing range and physical beauty, Taylor was spectacularly successful…"
- Leonard Feather, Los Angeles Times, Playboy Jazz Festival

But rather than strengthening my position, the attention seemed to make things worse. I could sense that Dan didn't like that I was stealing the light. So the emotional stress for me bubbled like molten metal underneath my "face". Being a quintessential American girl at heart, I struggled with my Western side, which wanted to go head-to-head with the challenge of the situation. Therefore, a hidden, turbulent energy existed between Dan and me, both of us wanting recognition and control. Not only was I dealing with an abusive husband at home, but I had a domineering boss to contend with.

I made one record with Hiroshima on Epic Records called East. We toured extensively for that record, and I did have the fulfilling pleasure of performing many wonderful shows with them. Aside from everything else, I enjoyed that aspect of performing as their lead singer. We did shows at venues like the Greek Theater, the Hollywood Bowl, Wolf Trap, Avery Fisher Hall at Lincoln Center, and at that level and size of performance spaces around the country. It wasn't stadiums and arenas, but there was an elegance and intimacy to playing those kinds of concert venues that I hadn't experienced in the larger settings.

A few years into my tenure, as Hiroshima began to work on another album, Bobby Columby, who was the president of Epic at the time, felt that I didn't sound black enough. Discrimination? Indeed. Anyway, it was the nascent period of the popularization of singers bombarding songs with melismatic riffing and vocal gymnastics, which, for me, is so overdone and not my thing. But that's what Bobby wanted for the band. With Bobby Columby overseeing the project and his vision, along with the strained relationship between Dan and me, we discontinued our contract and parted ways. In looking back, I wish it had happened sooner.

Regarding the other members of the band, Kimo Cornwall (keys), Dean Cortez (bass), Danny Yamamoto (drums), and Johnny Mori (taiko) were all skillful players, and lovely to work with. I have fond memories of working with them. I felt respected and supported by them. I believe they understood the dynamics between Dan and me, but were powerless to do anything about it. Nevertheless, it was a memorable opportunity to step to the front of the stage and enjoy a sense of my own musical power in that position as an artist. It was validating and liberating in many ways.

While it wasn't really where I wanted to be musically, singing with Hiroshima gave me a taste of being in community with other Japanese Americans for the first time. Even with the internal politics, it was a worthwhile experiment. And I am very grateful for the experience and what it taught me.

I think the big realization for me was that it solidified the fact that I am not, have never been, and will never be a traditional Japanese woman like my mother. I am an American woman with Japanese roots. Everything I worked for throughout my life was to break away from the subservient, second-rate citizen role that I witnessed my mother contend with. Unfortunately, that stigma is battled by many women around the world to this day. And that ideology seems to be frighteningly inching its way back in America thanks to certain factions. It's clear to me now that I should never acquiesce to any man or situation that would relegate me to anything less than what I feel I deserve, even in the face of my own internal struggles.

More importantly, my time with Hiroshima was an initiation of the process of reclaiming parts of my ethnic background that I had tried to conceal psychologically and emotionally for years. There were parts of me that I was made to feel shame about as a child in America. However, once again, I see how that experience was a necessary step in my personal evolution.

So there it was in a nutshell. My psychic push-pull, the emotional tightrope I was destined to walk: not feeling good enough for the white man's or black man's world, living in between worlds in a kind of perdition, but having the great desire to fit in and make something of myself. That was my quest for growth beyond my ancestral past. That was my spiritual Hiroshima… the pursuit to rise out of the ashes.

l - r: JUNE KURAMOTO - Koto; DANNY YAMAMOTO - Drums; DAN KURAMOTO - Keyboards, Woodwinds; JOHNNY MORI - Taiko, Percussion; MACHUN - Vocals, Guitar

HIROSHIMA

Los Angeles Times Review-Playboy Jazz Festival 1990

Los Angeles Times
TUESDAY, JUNE 19, 1990

Etta James at the Bowl: Welcome to Earplug City.

JAZZ REVIEW
A High-Decibel High at Playboy Festival

By LEONARD FEATHER

Hugh Hefner was clearly happy. Producer George Wein beamed. Bill Cosby, always eager to be part of the action, sat in on percussion with Hiroshima. Their enthusiasm fanned out to almost 18,000 patrons at Sunday's 8½-hour Playboy Jazz marathon at the Hollywood Bowl.

More than the Saturday session, this program leaned toward various forms of fusion. At one point Etta James remarked: "I know this is a jazz festival, I don't know what I'm doing here." But the honking and shouting of James and her so-called Roots Band was supposed to be a crowd killer first and a critic pleaser last.

Judged on its own R&B terms, the James vulgarisms had as logical a place here as Chick Corea's Elektric Band with its sometimes too spaced-out material, or the rockier moments of Hiroshima or Lee Ritenour. True, the Bowl too often became Earplug City, but the validity of the music, pure or hybridized, was seldom at issue.

Hiroshima came on late in the evening to bring the crowd to a rare pitch of frenzy with its Asian rock bombast. The key contributors were Johnny Mori, locked in mortal battle with a big taiko drum, June Okida Kuramoto in her exotic koto solos and, most memorably, the band's latest addition, a singer named Machun Taylor. Blessed with a

Drummer Bill Cosby, pianist Dorothy Donegan step out.

powerful voice, astonishing range and physical beauty, Taylor was spectacularly successful, most notably on a theme song in unison with Dan Kuramoto's saxophone.

Six hours earlier, the program had been launched with the Hennessy Jazz Search winner, a band known as Happy House that eschewed funk and fusion to concentrate on contemporary concepts in a post-Ornette Coleman acoustic vein.

Dorothy Donegan, a highly skilled pianist who was encouraged by no less an admirer than Art Tatum, showed her harmonic sense in "Here's That Rainy Day," her speed (verging on haste) in "Caravan," her swinging ease on "Isn't She Lovely," and her blues sensitivity on "After Hours." On this last she was joined by a young violinist, Laura Canaan, who played well but outstayed her welcome, interfering on tunes for which Donegan clearly wanted no assistance.

The white bearded Gerry Mulligan differed little from the adventurous young redhead who turned small-group jazz around in the 1950s. His creative impulses are as keen as they were back there when melody and harmony were

Please see FESTIVAL, F4

The Flip Side of Miles

"I would rather play new bad shit, rather than old good shit" - Miles Davis

In June of 1990, on tour in the States with Hiroshima, we were booked at the infamous then-named Avery Fischer Hall at Lincoln Center. The hall was renamed David Geffen Hall in 2015 because of his generous donation of $100 million dollars for renovations. Anyway, it was a big night for the band, playing this very prestigious venue in NYC, opening for Miles Davis.

Since I had had that memorable hang with Miles back in Nice when I toured with George Benson, I looked forward to possibly having a chance to say hello to him at some point that day. I thought there might be a chance to have a picture with him as well. But this was way before smartphones and the convenience of having a portable camera in your pocket. Capturing these moments in time was not as easy as it is now.

I remember Dan, and all of us, were pretty anxious about our performance that night. After all, opening for Miles in this legendary hall, which was the home of the New York Philharmonic Orchestra and hailed performances by the greats of classical, jazz, and contemporary music, was amazing. It was considered a pinnacle point in one's career. I think it still is.

The soundcheck that day was stressful. The hall at that time was boomy, and not acoustically friendly to electronic instruments. It's not what it was designed for originally. I recall there was quite a bit of slapback. But as many of you may know, soundchecking a room without an audience is hugely different from the sound with a full house of people. The amount of sound that gets absorbed by bodies in the room means that the front-of-house mix can change drastically.

I recall Dan not being happy with the soundcheck or setlist. I think he was disturbed by how my voice, in particular, was bouncing loudly around the venue. But that could have been my sensitivity, because he decided to pull an important song of mine from the set called 'Come to Me'.

I remember being really upset about Dan pulling that song. When I walked off the stage after soundcheck, I felt my wings had been clipped, and felt a gut-burning sense of anger toward him. I think he knew it. Perhaps we were both fighting ghosts.

This particular incident is something I've seen in the music business time and time again. There are some artists who are enlivened by surrounding themselves with talented people who help elevate them, their band, and the show. To me, it makes the music better and is better for the audience. If you're secure about your own talents and with what you have to offer, there's no need to feel threatened.

On the other hand, there are artists and band leaders who do whatever they can to keep the people around them in their place, so as not to steal the show. It's small-minded and doesn't allow for the art and performance to flourish. At that moment, I felt that was what was happening to me. Not that I thought I was so great. But the opportunity to shine and relish that moment, performing at Avery Fisher, was being crushed.

Honestly, I don't remember whether I convinced Dan to let me perform that song or not. But I do remember this…

After Miles soundchecked his band, there was time for dinner and some leeway before showtime. So I sought out his dressing room. I found Gordon, who was still working for Miles as his personal valet, and exchanged niceties with him for a bit. Then I asked if he would take me to say hello to Miles. He agreed and led me into his dressing room.

The room was a hub of activity, with musicians warming up, chatting, and hanging out. Miles was in B-line view, seated on a large sofa, holding court. There was a very distinct male energy dominating the room, like the smell of sharp musk. I felt in my gut that it might not be a good time to come into that space, but I just wanted to steal a quick flash of a moment to pay my respects and say hello. I banked on a romantic notion that Miles would remember me and that lovely exchange we had back in Nice. And that it would buy me admission to a moment of his time.

As I approached the sofa, clearly Miles was not in a good mood. He looked up at me and Gordon and said to Gordon, "Who is this?" Then he kind of grumbled some unintelligible objections, and said, "Get this bitch out of here!" Classic!

I was taken aback, but at the same time laughed, because Miles was famously known to be moody, unpredictable, and even mean. I remember Gordon was kind of flustered, and just looked at me to turn around and leave.

I was momentarily hurt that Miles addressed me as he did. But I knew it wasn't personal. He was just being himself. Either he didn't remember me, or he just wasn't in the mood. I got it. He was, after all, one of the greatest jazz musicians of all time. That afforded him a bit of an excuse in my mind.

In the end, Miles, being the great artist that he was, was all about creating new ideas and moving forward. He was an innovator. A genius of his time. He was about taking risks and leaving the past behind. So, of course, as I see it now, I was just a tiny blip on his radar. For him, I was most likely a relic of the past, old shit, and a distant memory. He had moved far beyond my little moment in time with him in France.

It was still an incredible honor to share the stage with him that night at Avery Fisher Hall. It was a sold out show, and a great night for both Hiroshima and Miles' band. All and all, a new feather in my cap, and a funny memory. Priceless.

Calendar of Events
AVERY FISHER HALL LINCOLN CENTER
June 1990

1 Friday 8pm
NEW YORK PHILHARMONIC
Erich Leinsdorf, conductor
Mahler: Symphony No. 7, "Song of the Night"
$40 to $10

2 Saturday 8pm
NEW YORK PHILHARMONIC
Same as June 1

3 Sunday 4pm
G CLEF CORPORATION
& FRIENDS in Concert
Take Six and a 70 Piece Chimes Children Choir, N. J. Mass Choir and others
$35

5 Tuesday 8:30pm
IN CONCERT FOR ONE PEOPLE
For information call (212)279-2525

8 Friday 8pm
An evening with
LINDA RONSTADT
for the benefit of the T. J. Martell Foundation for Leukemia, Cancer & Aids Research
$35

14 Thursday 8pm
GEORGE WINSTON
$25, $22.50, $20

15 Friday 8pm
GEORGE WINSTON
Same as June 14.

16 Saturday 7:30pm
RUTH WILLIAMS DANCE STUDIO RECITAL
$15, $13, $11

22 Friday 7pm/11pm
JVC Jazz Festival
MILES DAVIS & HIROSHIMA
$35, $30, $25, $17.50

23 Saturday 8pm
JVC Jazz Festival
LEE RITENOUR / PATTI AUSTIN & NEW YORK VOICES
$30, $25, $20, $17.50

24 Sunday 7pm/11pm
JVC Jazz Festival
RAY CHARLES & ROBERTA FLACK
$35, $30, $25, $17.50

26 Tuesday 8pm
JVC Jazz Festival
MILTON NASCIMENTO & WAYNE SHORTER
$30, $25, $20 $17.50

27 Wednesday 8pm
JVC Jazz Festival
PEARL BAILEY
WYNTON MARSALIS
$40, $30, $25, $17.50

28 Thursday 8pm
JVC Jazz Festival
REGINA BELLE
THE HARPER BROTHERS
$30, $27.50, $22.50, $17.50

29 Friday 8pm
JVC Jazz Festival
ELLA FITZGERALD
$50, $40, $30, $17.50

30 Saturday 8pm
JVC Jazz Festival
Jazz Mobile Benefit: 25th ANNIVERSARY OF JAZZMOBILE
NANCY WILSON
AHMAD JAMAL TRIO
TERENCE BLANCHARD QUINTET
$30, $25, $20, $17.50

LINCOLN CENTER'S MOSTLY MOZART
begins July 10 and continues through August 25

Tickets at box office (212)874-2424 or call:
CenterCharge (212)874-6770

What You Won't Do For Love - Bobby Caldwell

"Every man is more than just himself; he also represents the unique, the very special and always significant and remarkable point at which the world's phenomena intersect, only once in this way, and never again" - Hermann Hesse

Coming out of the blunder with Hiroshima, I went back to being a background singer with one of the most talented singer/songwriter/musicians I've known, Bobby Caldwell. Bobby had more talent in his pinky finger than most. And for someone like that, it can be a huge blessing or a little bit of a curse.

For those that don't know, Bobby's big claim to fame is the song 'What You Won't Do For Love', released in 1979. The now classic song has a badass groove, great melody and infectious hook. Bobby wrote and played pretty much everything on that recording, as he often did on his records. Everyone thought he was black when that song hit the charts, because of his soulful vocals and that sexy groove. And if you just listened to his music, you could happily exist with an Afro-American idea of him. But the reality of his skinny white man look, in truth, may have been detrimental to his career in the end. Who knows.

The category of "blue-eyed soul" in the music business was coined in the 1960s, referring to white artists who sounded like African American artists. The term was quite derogatory for some. And for Bobby, I think it may have been a sticking point. Nevertheless, Bobby had many hits in the 1980s and 90s that he wrote for other artists, like Peter Cetera, Boz Scaggs, Natalie Cole, Al Jarreau, Neil Diamond, and others. He was a noted songwriter behind the scenes. But he had always longed to have his own identity as an artist.

When I met Bobby, around 1990, he was getting ready to gear up for a tour in Japan, where he was a bit of a star. They called him "Mister AOR", which stands for Adult Oriented Rock. It's equivalent to the Adult Contemporary charts in the US. The Japanese are so appreciative of real talent in all genres of music. I think there's a deeper appreciation for more sophisticated American artists in other countries; that's why so many jazz musicians can forge careers in Japan and Europe, with little support from the US. I don't know why. Anyway, it was just what I needed to shift gears after stalling out from the previous career left turn.

My old friend Allen Hinds, a great guitarist who had played with Hiroshima for a stint, referred me to Bobby when he was looking for a background vocalist. Allen would be doing the tour and thought I'd be a good fit. I remember talking to Bobby for the first time. He was so sweet and welcoming. And he loved the fact that I was half Japanese, which he thought would bode well for his tour in Japan.

Working with Bobby was a delight because the music was so richly written and arranged, yet still pop, with strong, memorable choruses. He always had great hooks, and great vocal parts for us background singers. However, the fact that Bobby was an accomplished multi-instrumentalist made it arduous at times, I think, for some band members. Bobby knew exactly what he wanted to hear on every instrument and every arrangement; he had it all well thought out. Even when he had musicians play on his records, he might end up replacing their parts with his own. He had such a strong musical sensibility, and always knew what he wanted. Perhaps some of that vigilant oversight came from a need to be in control too. But it came primarily from his impeccable sense of himself as an artist and his musical taste. Therein lies that little hidden curse that comes with that kind of talent and a sense of control.

The first tour with Bobby was with band members Allen Hinds (guitar), George Perelli (drums), Jimmy Haslip (drums), Debra Dobkin (percussion/vox), Joe Turrano (keys), Bobby Martin (keys), and Dan Pelfree (sax). Not a shabby player in the bunch.

For the following tour, in 1991, Bobby wanted to make some changes, and a few people weren't available. So Allen, George, Debra and I stayed on, with some new members: Boney James (sax), Roberto Vally (bass), Michael James (keys/vocals), Tollak Olstead (keys/vox), and the wonderful Marilyn Scott (vocals) joined the crew. Marilyn, who also had a solo career of her own, was featured on a duet with Bobby in the show.

Going back to Japan with Bobby was very different than my experiences with previous tours I did. Bobby's fans were a mix of young and old, pop and jazz, and those fans who knew his songs through other artists that he had written for. The venues we played were dignified, medium-sized theaters that carried an air of Radio City Music Hall excitement about them.

As with my previous tours to Japan, my cousin Akio Sasaki would always come to see me, with his friend Yoko Arikawa. Yoko spoke very good English and would interpret for us. I always felt sorry for her, as she had to work hard volleying back and forth between Akio and me in two different languages. But I know how close they were, and they seemed to get a kick out of my visits and musical adventures.

Akio and I are just a year or so apart in age and knew each other as young children when I lived in Japan. When I met up with him during my visits as an adult, it was as if we fell right back into the family feeling. The saying "blood is thicker than water" resonated with me when I saw him. Even though we had spent many years apart and dealt with a language barrier, there was always that inherent connection that was comfortable, as only family can be.

The great benefit of having Akio as my tour guide in Japan was that he would take me to restaurants and places in Tokyo that only locals would know. Once, on a day off, he took me and Yoko up to what I recall was the Naeba Ski Resort area, not far from Tokyo. It wasn't ski season, but it was a beautiful ride and a much-needed diversion from the tour. We visited a bathhouse in that region and went to a fabulous restaurant. I don't remember the names of these places. But the food in Japan was spectacular; even the little hole-in-the-wall places would serve the freshest, most delicious dishes. Nothing like what I've had in America. I'll never forget those off-the-beaten-path adventures with Akio, which made those trips so special for me.

After those two big tours to Japan with Bobby and a string of shows around the States, I left Los Angeles in 1994. It was hard to disconnect from my West Coast friends, and musicians I had developed relationships with. But flash forward to around 2014, Bobby and I reconnected in New York. He had re-married and was living in New Jersey with his new wife Mary. He wanted to have a band based out of the East Coast and a band based on the West Coast for budgetary reasons.

I rejoined his East Coast band for a few years, working places like the Blue Note in NYC and Scullers in Boston. It was a far cry from the big, first-class theater shows, TV, and scads of fans in Japan. But it was a still a thrill to sing those songs with him again and reconstitute our friendship.

Sadly, Bobby passed in March 14th, 2023. He slowly deteriorated after suffering severe side effects from taking the antibiotic fluoroquinolone in 2017. I think it was a slow and painful downslope for him. Honestly, if I had known about how horrid his situation was, I would have gone to visit him during his decline. But like the rest of the world, I had no idea about what he had been going through, and was shocked and saddened when he passed. What was particularly disturbing about his passing was knowing that he had unnecessarily suffered from a rare and bizarre medical debacle. It was a tragic end for the brilliant, creative and kind soul that he was. His fervid musical spirit is greatly missed. But his one-of-a-kind musical imprint will thankfully be ours forever.

(left to right)
Tollack Olsted, Boney James, Allen Hinds, Debra Dobkin,
Bobby Caldwell and me
Tokyo 1991

Bobby Caldwell and me, Tokyo 1991

Exodus East

"It's a funny thing coming home. Nothing changes. Everything looks the same, feels the same, even smells the same. You realize what's changed is you" - F.Scott Fitzgerald

Packing up all my belongings and upending my life again in 1994 was no easy decision. I had lived in Los Angeles for a little over a decade. It had been a good chunk out of my prime thirties. But I needed to leave behind the destructive aftermath of my first marriage, which should have been dissolved a few years earlier. And truth be told, my East Coast/New York soul never entirely felt at home in LA. So, I made my exodus back east.

I landed living in a loft downtown on Wooster St that my ex had been keeping for his bi-coastal work purposes. It was awkward being there while we started our divorce proceedings, but I was grateful to have a comfortable, rent-free place to be while I tried to regain my footing in the concrete jungle. Making this move was one of the hardest transitions of my life. I knew it was the best thing I could do for myself, my safety, and my sanity. But even knowing all that, I still felt completely gutted and a loathsome failure. It's funny how I was subconsciously afflicted with the Christian belief that divorce is somehow a defeat or a sin, no matter how unsound and untenable a situation.

This to me, speaks like the convoluted opinion about abortion for some people of religious inclination. Just because a woman is pregnant doesn't mean it's a good idea to have the baby if doing so endangers her life or that of the baby. And what about rape? Then on a purely practical level, what if it's not an opportune time to bring another precious, fully dependent human being into the world? What if a woman isn't able or capable of caring for the development of that life beyond the stage of a fetus? It's a huge responsibility that should be taken seriously. But I digress.

One of the saving graces at the time of my leaving LA was the Buddhist practice I was introduced to by the late great Wayne Shorter and his beautiful wife Ana. Ana tragically died in the infamous TWA flight 800 plane crash in 1996. Both Wayne and Ana brought me into the practice of Nichiren Buddhism at the moment when I really needed strength to change my reality drastically.

Wayne had seen me perform at the Playboy Jazz Festival in 1990 with the band Hiroshima. He liked my voice, and made the effort to find me through mutual friends and my accountant. I was so honored to be invited to his house to discuss the possibility of being included on his next record at that time. I was blown away! It was a distinct highlight in my life to be acknowledged by a brilliant music legend such as he was.

For those of you that don't know who Wayne Shorter was, he was an innovative jazz saxophonist, whose career spanned from the 1950s to the 2020s. He played with Art Blakey's Jazz Messengers, and The Miles Davis Quintet in the early days. And he went on to co-found the incredible jazz, rock, fusion group Weather Report with Joe Zawinul. Beyond that, his own brilliant solo records and compositions are part of the pantheon of jazz music history.

When I first met Wayne and Ana, they were living in LA, over the hill from Laurel Canyon. The day I visited their home, the house bustled with friends of Ana's and workers attending to the needs of their business office and home. After formalities and introductions, Wayne sat me down next to him on the bench in front of his beautiful grand piano, like being seated on a pew before an altar. He generously proceeded to bring alive the entire score, and I do mean score. Pages and pages of a magnificent musical tapestry that was scotch taped together, strewn across the piano, unfolded in front of me. It was his next creation. And he was sharing it with me. He enthusiastically spoke of cosmology, science, spirituality, nature, life, and a depth of imagery he associated with and channeled through his music. It was deep. Deeper than any musical exchange I've ever had with anyone. Probably even more profound than I could comprehend at the time. I was awestruck. I knew I was in the presence of a true master artist of the highest standing.

Before I left his house that day, he invited me to chant with him and Ana. Chant? It seemed a little weird, and I wasn't sure what he meant. But I trusted that whatever it was, it was sure to be interesting. He led me to a special room in his house dedicated to a gigantic Gohonzon and altar. A Gohonzon is a calligraphic mandala of sorts. An object of devotion. It represents the Mystic Law of the Lotus Sutra, honored in Nichiren Buddhism.

As we entered the room, meditation pillows were strewn about in front of the Gohonzon. There was seating enough to accommodate a small group of people comfortably. He instructed me to just sit and listen while he and Ana performed their evening prayers. They ceremoniously rang the brass bowl, lit the candle, and burned incense on the altar to signal the start of prayer time. I felt this mystical energy infuse the room. When they started chanting, the sound and vibrations from their voices seemed to magically energize the molecules of my body in a spellbinding way. It was music. It made my skin tingle and my heart open. I was inspired to learn more. I somehow knew instinctively it was what I needed.

Wayne graciously invited me back to his house several times after that day. Each time, I was introduced a little more to this curious sound of Namu Myōhō Renge Kyō. Little by little, I began to learn the Daimoku (prayers) and more about the Lotus Sutra those prayers are based on. Not long after, I received my own Gohonzon, and I was formally initiated into the practice.

Ultimately, I didn't get to sing on Wayne's record after Marcus Miller came in to produce it. But the enduring gift that Wayne and Ana gave me was their warm support and the practice of Nichiren Buddhism, which radically changed my life. It helped me find the strength to leave a bad situation, take responsibility for my own happiness, and reclaim my existence. I will forever be grateful to them for their generous and loving guidance.

Letter from Ana Shorter to me before she died

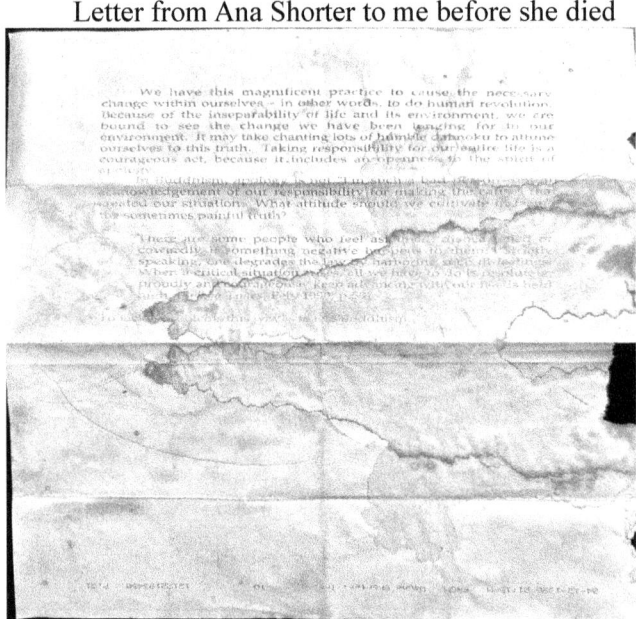

'We have this magnificent practice to cause the necessary change within ourselves- in other words, to do human revolution. Because of the inseprability of life and its environment, we are bound to see the change we have been longing for in our environment. It may take chanting lots of humble daimoku to attune ourselves to this truth. Taking responsibility for our entire life is a courageous act because it includes a spirit of apology.

In Buddhism, apology is not ' I'm such a bad person', but an acknowledgement of our resposibility for making the causes that created our situation. What attitude should we cultivate in facing the sometimes painful truth?

There are some people who feel ashamed, disheartened or cowardly if something negative happens to them. Strictly speaking, one degrades the law by harboring such ill feelings. When a critical situation arises, all we have to do is resolutely, proudly and courageously keep advancing with our heads held high. (Seikyo Times, Feb 1990, p. 59)

To tackle problems this way is to live Buddhism.

Love, Ana

Panic at the Deposition

"Our anxiety does not come from thinking about the future, but from wanting to control it"— Kahlil Gibran

The divorce proceedings with Bruno were not going well. The fact that I declared that there was emotional and physical abuse during the marriage required that I produce some kind of evidence to substantiate my case. Luckily, I was able to obtain letters from doctors, therapists, and friends with supporting testimonies of what they witnessed, noted, and knew about my situation.

For example, when I was examined by an eye doctor after being punched and suffering a black eye that ruptured the membrane around my eye, the eye doctor had kept a record of that. I endured fractured ribs another time. I ended up with a broken finger after another ugly confrontation. I had photographs of me with bruises that were clearly not self-inflicted. Gosh, when I see those pictures now, I don't know who that bewildered-looking woman is.

The scars of emotional abuse in these situations always lie hidden beneath the surface, out of the light of day, and are challenging to prove. They are deeply damaging and embarrassing. The therapist I was working with at the time was able to confirm to the lawyers how injurious the effects of my ex's behavior were on me, and how the marriage was destroying me.

Bruno tried to deny it all. He never really admitted wrongdoing or owned any responsibility. In fact, he thought that whatever ill behavior he acted out on me was provoked by me. That somehow it was all my fault. That is classic abuser's rationale. And the fact that I dared to surrender and make our story public infuriated him even more. It blew the lid off his ego and his cover. So, I had to file a restraining order against him.

On the outside, I don't think a lot of people realized the suffering I had been going through in that marriage, except for a few close friends. There may have been a few instances where someone heard us arguing in a hotel room or witnessed his angry and controlling ways with me. However, overall, I suspect the general public was oblivious. That, too, is very typical of abusive relationships. The truth is usually lurking in the shadows and behind closed doors. In some cases, for the unfortunate few, it's revealed to the public only when it's too late.

The separation and divorce proceedings had been going on for about a year when I was called to appear at a deposition in Los Angeles. So I flew back west and stayed with Marcene and Danny, who were living in Westlake Village then. The proceeding was to take place in Century City, which, depending on traffic, would take me at least an hour to drive to. You never know in LA, and it usually takes longer than you think.

On the day of the deposition, I jumped into my rental car with plenty of time to comfortably make it there before the meeting. I felt wired, as if I had been doing speed, riddled with anxiety, though externally I was holding it together reasonably well. I remember I was dressed casually in a size six pair of beige checkered summer dress pants and a nice dressy T-shirt. I was at my lowest weight ever in my adult life: skinny and somewhat gaunt from the stress.

I vividly recall traveling on the 101 Freeway around Sherman Oaks when I suddenly became aware that I was claustrophobically surrounded by three big MACK trailer trucks. We were barreling down the freeway in procession together, and I was frighteningly trapped in the middle of them like a cornered animal. I couldn't breathe. My hands started to feel sickly, sweaty, and weak. I wasn't sure I could hang on to the steering wheel. My heart was pounding out of rhythm to the surface of my chest, almost breaking the skin. My breath was shortening and constricting more and more with every tenth of a mile.

At first, I thought I might be having a heart attack. I had been under a lot of stress after all, so I imagined it possible. But I was pretty healthy and too young, I thought. As the fear and shock began to overwhelm me, I started to talk to myself out loud. "Machan, you need to get away from these trucks and get to the side of the road. Take your foot off the gas so you can slow down and fall behind these guys. You're gonna be ok." Feeling suffocated under the unbearable weight of my panic, I rolled down the windows, even though the air conditioning was blasting, and it was LA desert hot outside. I thought moving air would help me breathe.

As I took my foot off the gas, I started to slow down, to the bewilderment of the cars behind me. Even with my body and mind feeling paralyzed, somehow, in an out-of-body way, I could sense the big tractor-trailers gradually rolling forward away from me, clearing some space between us and my view of the lanes to my right and to the side of the road. I started chanting, "Get off the road Machan, get off the road." Feeling completely out of my mind at this point, I was drenched in sweat and the palpitations were taking a "Wipe Out" drum solo in my chest. I don't remember how my hands were able to steer the car, but I miraculously managed to swing right across a few lanes and landed at the shoulder of the freeway.

When the car stopped, I dropped my forehead to the steering wheel in sheer relief, breathlessly thanking the gods for protecting me and keeping me from a horrible car crash. To this day, I don't know how I managed to control the car. I feel certain that it was some kind of divine intervention, a guardian angel, or my grandmother looking over me.

As I started gathering my breath and thoughts, I felt like I should call someone for help. So I called my therapist in NYC for some strange reason, rather than 911. I don't know why, but I instinctively knew it was a matter of mind rather than body. Shockingly, my therapist picked up the phone, which had never happened before.

In a high-pitched, frantic voice, I reported to my therapist the details of the drama that had just played out for me on the freeway. He silently listened to the unfolding of my report, and when I finished, he calmly and assuredly said, "Oh Machan, you've just had a classic panic attack. It happens to a lot of people in various ways. But I think given your circumstance, it's perfectly understandable. You're going to be ok."

Part of me was relieved to hear him say that. But the other part of me felt a little disappointed that there wasn't something terribly wrong with me, and I couldn't check myself into the hospital and avoid going to the deposition. I was going to be ok? How could that be when I just felt like I was going to die? Why, then, was I feeling like a spineless wet noodle, with no sense of life and no ability to move? It took me a little while to grasp the concept of a panic attack. And why it was happening to me.

After my therapist reassured me that I would survive this harrowing episode, and I would be able to regain my composure, I remembered I had to get myself to Century City, which was still twenty minutes away with traffic. I didn't know how I was going to make it, but I knew I couldn't stay on the freeway. I was too shaken up to stay that course. So I exited from where I was and got onto the surface roads, which I knew really well. After having spent a decade living in LA, I could weave myself through back and side streets enough to still get to the meeting in time.

I don't remember much about the details of the deposition that day other than it was humiliating to sit in the same room as my ex, and have details of my marriage and life strewn thoughtlessly across a large conference table, with strange male lawyers to whom I was just another case number, and another tragic story in the world of a fifty percent divorce rate in the US. Already jolted by my panic attack as if I had been electrocuted, I had to use every bit of strength in that meeting to not melt into a puddle of tears in front of everyone.

Needing to return to Westlake Village that afternoon, I limped the car back in the right-hand lane of the freeway, going as slowly as possible. It was torturous. I pissed off a lot of other drivers that day. As I sat in a sunken-down posture, with my arms stretched up on the steering wheel, people probably thought, "Oh, that stupid old Asian lady doesn't know how to drive." Moreover, I knew I would never again feel the same about driving. Even though I had enjoyed operating a car since I was sixteen, without ever having an accident or a moving violation, my relationship with this independent act of propulsion through life was forever changed.

After returning to NYC, I didn't drive again for some seven years. Luckily, living in NYC, I didn't need to. After that long absence, the time arrived when I wanted to travel on my own again. I wanted to take gigs out of town and regain that sense of freedom and adventure that comes with getting behind the wheel. I eventually managed to reacquaint myself with driving again, with the help of some hypnosis and therapy. It worked pretty well. But it's never been quite the same. Ever. My brain was deeply engraved with the ordeal of that day on the LA freeway. Like an elephant never forgetting. Or red wine spilled on a pure white carpet—there's a faint, but permanent stain.

Back in the Big Apple

"Home isn't where you're from, it's where you find light when all grows dark" — Pierce Brown

Not having been established in NYC since 1984, a lot had changed in terms of the music scene, the economy, and the landscape of the lifestyle of being a real city dweller in the Big Apple. Soho, which was once a deserted industrial wasteland, was once occupied by only bohemian artists and musicians. In the 1970s and 80s they reclaimed funky, rundown leftover warehouses from the era of the mercantile and dry goods industry of the late 1800s. Long before that, it was the first free Black settlement in Manhattan, where freed slaves were given farmland to work. Now, it was becoming a high-end shopping area with expensive restaurants trampled by tourists. By the time I returned, the rents were already out of control.

After spending a lot of time in a pool of pity in fetal position on the floor, I eventually pulled the broken pieces of myself back together in kintsugi fashion. For anyone who doesn't know, the art of kintsugi is an ancient Japanese craft that serves as a metaphor for life. It's the art of mending broken pottery with gold. It teaches us to see that there is character and beauty in mending the fragmented parts of ourselves. It's an opportunity to heal, build fortitude and assimilate the riches learned from the difficulties in life.

Step by step, I began to emerge from my cocoon to join the sweeping fast lane of life again in New York City. I gradually started getting recording sessions and club date gigs in town. I was running on the Westside walkway four to five days a week. I got into really good physical shape, even though I could feel the disruptive symptoms of peri-menopause coming on. Change was in the air, in my body, and in my life.

Over the next few years of revamping what felt like a discombobulated Picasso portrait of myself, I knew I was healing from the melodrama of six years with the wrong guy in the wrong place. Therapy and damage control were central activities of my days. I felt at home again in my skin and in the city. The symbolic anchoring of my mother living in New Jersey in my childhood home also added ballast. I had gone full circle like a Saturn return.

With doing more recording sessions in town, I befriended Rick DePofi and Craig Bishop, who were just starting a new jingle company called New York Noise. They had started their work out of Rick's apartment on Sullivan Street just down the block from the apartment where I ended up after my divorce. They were in the middle of constructing a beautiful, brand-new facility on Gansevoort Street. I started hanging out with Rick and Craig and their circle of friends for dinners and drinks. My world was expanding and opening up. It was the beginning of a wonderful, new chapter in Gotham.

Getting back into a musical life, I reconnected with some old musician friends, including Steve Gaboury, a keyboard player/composer and great guy who I had known since the late 1970s. We had collaborated on various music library and personal projects. And we always had a great time together. I was very comfortable working with him and trusted his musical taste, so he helped me with some new song demos. Also, in addition, I had other material that I had compiled back in LA. When I had enough for a little label presentation, I threw a demo package together and presented it to some people I knew. I reached out to Ed Gerard, who was also back in NY. Ed had been part of the management team with Daniel Marcus at Shep Gordon's office in LA. They had managed Hiroshima when I was with them. I thought surely the weight of Shep Gordon's name would be helpful.

Shep had managed and developed the careers of Alice Cooper, Luther Vandross, and Teddy Pendegrass. And he had other successes in the film industry. He was a well-known heavy hitter in the music industry, which benefited Ed and Daniel's clout as well. Anyway, Ed agreed to shop my demo package. Miraculously, he landed me a little development deal with Bruce Lundvall at Blue Note Records right off the bat.

Bruce awarded me a $5000 budget to record a few songs that would represent to him a concept of how I saw myself as an artist, and perhaps convince him to sign me to a record deal. I recorded three songs: one with Rick DePofi, one with Steve Gaboury, and the last with Steve Miller. The budget afforded us to have some great New York session players, in combination with digitally programmed arrangements.

I thought the recordings turned out really well. They embodied a kind of jazz/pop sensibility that suited me well; some harmonic sophistication, and songs with hooks. But as enthusiastic and receptive as Bruce was about my presentation, he didn't end up signing me. I think he signed Patricia Barber at the time. It was a transitional period for the Blue Note label and its identity. It was the period just before the label shifted its focus to a more pop-oriented direction with the signing of Nora Jones. And their incredible legacy catalog took a back seat.

Regardless of the outcome, interacting with the legendary Bruce Lundvall, who was one of the last of that generation of powerhouse gentlemen in the business, was a marked moment. That episode inspired me to get back into songwriting and playing out again, which was a passion I had lost when I was married to Bruno.

Step by step, I poked my way back to a semblance of my former self, with the added depth and dimension that came from the life experiences I had collected during my decade living in LA.

This new avenue of my life would lead me to unimagined personal and professional opportunities. I truly believe it was because I dared to risk giving up everything I had and dove into the abyss.

JAZZ AND CLASSICS, CAPITOL RECORDS

BRUCE LUNDVALL

Dear Machan

I like this. You sound great & the song is dark & interesting. Thanks for sending to me. I think you're on the right track!

Best,
Bruce

Out of the Blue

"A person often meets his destiny on the road he took to avoid it" - Jean de La Fontaine

It's said that the best relationships happen when you're not looking. They happen when you're feeling fulfilled and happy within yourself and you own your own life. Looking back on when I met Danny, I know this to be true.

The first few years of me being back in NYC, I was focused primarily on taking care of my physical and mental health. I knew I needed a lot of time to heal from the trauma of my previous marriage, and needed time to face the exploratory work of analyzing my personal history and the psychology that had allowed me to end up where I did. It was a slow, arduous effort that I knew needed to happen if I were going to emerge a healthier and happier person.

At first, I was seeing an individual therapist, who, when I look back, may not have been the right person equipped to handle my situation. But he was kind and affordable. I think I spent a lot of time wallowing in self-pity before I got to core issues enough to make some real change. But I know you get it when you're ready. There is no rushing the process.

After a while, I found myself in group therapy and a 12-step program for adult children of alcoholics. The value of both modalities is that you realize you're not alone in your misery. And in fact, as the case was for me, I found out that other people had far more horrendous stories and far worse trauma than I did. That kind of perspective helped to transform my almost neurotic narcissism and "woe is me" stance to a more expansive, curious, and compassionate position. There's nothing worse than being mesmerized by your own navel and not being able to see the world around you. It's such a contracted state.

Unfortunately, psychedelic-assisted therapy was not a widely known option at that time. If I had known about it then, I think it would have sped up my healing process tenfold. In the dozen or so times I've had psychedelic journeys, I can say that they have been incredibly transformative sessions in a way that simple talk therapy has not been for me. That said, the integrative work that happens after a medicine journey is of major importance to the overall process. It's like with voice lessons. What happens between lessons is almost more important than the lesson itself. While gaining the tools of the skill during lessons is essential, it's what the student does with the information and how they apply it that's integral to their development. There is no one and done.

Anyway, circling back to my original thought, after almost three years of basically keeping to myself and not pursuing a relationship, out of the blue I met Danny. I was finally in a place where I felt good about myself again. I was in really good mental and physical shape. I had my dog. I had some work. I had creative projects going on. And I felt content in a way that I hadn't felt in a long time. Maybe never.

At some point in 1997, my friend Rick DePofi called me to come do a vocal session for him on a commercial demo. It was for a 7up commercial that featured a cartoon created by comedian and actor Robert Smigel. They were developing a concept styled after "The Ambiguously Gay Duo" cartoon of Smigel's titled "The 7up Thirst Twins". I don't think the concept ever flew, but the music was fun.

When I got to the studio for the session, this tall, thin, wiry, cute guy named Danny was a co-writer/co-producer of the commercial. Danny had recently started writing jingles for Rick and his partner Craig Bishop for their New York Noise studio. Norman Mershon was the other singer on the session.

Working with Rick and Danny was always an entertaining encounter. Rick's dark, sarcastic humor was somehow complemented by Danny's smart ass, twisted sensibility, making for funny banter and a jovial work environment. Moreover, they were dedicated to a professional work ethic and making good music. So the end result was always something to be proud of.

During that session, I definitely felt an attraction to this guy Danny, and I thought he might have felt the same about me. But being in a professional setting, neither one of us was in a position to act on those thoughts. At the end of the session, we parted ways not knowing when we would meet again.

A few months later, Rick was working with me on a song for my Blue Note development deal. Rick called Danny to visit and listen to what we were working on. I later learned that Rick had told Danny, "This chick is more than just a singer. She's a musician. I think you'll dig her stuff."

A little later, Danny rolled in on his bicycle, into the studio control room. Rick introduced Danny to me as one of his best friends in the world. I knew that it was significant for him to say that. I would later find out more about the importance of that statement. We smiled and recalled meeting each other on the 7up commercial and sat down on the studio couch.

Rick decided to go outside for a smoke break or make some calls and left Danny and me to talk for a bit. Our conversation was easy. He was chatty and funny and seemed very available to talk about anything. We covered everything. Danny says he remembers us talking about how long it had been since we both had sex. What? Funny that I don't remember that at all!

There was a spark of warmth I felt in that first meeting with Danny that I hadn't felt in a very long time. It was more than just sexual attraction or lust. It was a fresh sense that I could trust this person. That I could feel friendship, love, and safety with this man. I had the feeling that I might have a life with him, which was the last thing I was looking for.

As Rick and I were prepping for an overdub session, Danny departed from the studio, leaving me with a piqued interest and desire to see him again. But again, because we connected in a professional setting, we simply said goodbye. I looked forward to the next time I would see him.

Around September 30th of 1998, I was working with a friend of mine from Holland, Jaap Eggermont, on some commercial productions for him to take back to Amsterdam. We were working at my friend Steve Gaboury's studio. After Jaap and I had dinner, I took him to see Rick DePofi's band, Mojo Mancini, who were playing at the Gaslight club that used to be on 14th St.

Mojo Mancini comprised of John Leventhal on guitar, Brian Mitchell on keys, Shawn Pelton on drums, Conrad Korsch on bass, and Rick on horns and Omnichord. Another band iteration included Tony Garnier, of Bob Dylan notoriety, on bass. Overall, the appeal of the sound of the band was that they were all good friends, just wanting to make good music together. Collectively, their all-star credentials included recording and/or performing with the following artists: David Byrne, Rosanne Cash, Marc Cohn, Shawn Colvin, Elvis Costello, Sheryl Crow, Bob Dylan, Paul McCartney, Van Morrison, Willie Nelson, Joan Osborne, Rod Stewart, and many others.

I think it was basically Rick and John's concept of a noir, angular, rock, jazz, Hollywood film-inspired instrumental music. They kind of defied definition, which is what made them so cool. With the quality of the players in Mojo, it was always a great hang at their gigs. It was essentially the NY Noise community hang, happening at an exciting time in the city.

As Jaap and I settled into a seat with some drinks before the band started, Danny tumbled into the Gaslight with his friends Matt and Heather Carlson, bubbling with glee. They had just come from a Yankee playoff game, which the team had won. They were so excited about how well the Yankees were doing—rightfully so, as they went on to win the World Series a month or so later that year.

I introduced Jaap to Danny and his friends as the band started their first set. Jaap picked up on the energy between Danny and me and shot a knowing smile. He left after the first set to return to his hotel since he was jet-lagged and tired. On his way out, Jaap singingly said, "Have fun! See you tomorrow!" and left me to search for Danny.

I discovered Danny on his own as his friends had left after the first set of music as well. So we huddled up together and ordered a few drinks, positioning ourselves in front of the stage for Mojo's second set. I felt that same ease and warmth that I had remembered from his visit that day in the studio. But this time, we were in a social setting and free to write the script going forward.

When Mojo finished, we hung out for a while, chatting with Rick and many folks in that circle. I think that was the night I met the illustrious singer Elaine Caswell, Shawn Pelton's partner, who is still a good friend of mine. So many amazing New York musicians, singers, and creative people hung out at those gigs. It was a scene to be seen in.

When it was time to leave, Danny asked where I was going. He offered to walk me home. So in the late of the evening, with a gentle rain starting to fall, we walked arm and arm through the night. Still talking away, trying to find out as much about each other as we could; you could sense us both sussing out whether or not we were going to take the leap and explore this new territory of our hearts.

When we arrived at my apartment building, he didn't ask to come in, to my surprise. He asked for my phone number and inquired about what I was doing Friday night. We made a date to have dinner. Then I asked him if he liked opera. I had just purchased season tickets for the MET Opera as a gift to myself. He lied of course, and said he loved it. So we also planned to do that together in a few weeks.

Danny politely kissed me goodnight and made sure I got into my building. I floated up to my apartment in a blissful haze, smitten with this new, tantalizing promise of hope. My phone rang twenty minutes later as I was getting ready for bed. It was Danny, calling to say goodnight and say what a nice time he had had. I was so tickled that he made that effort.

We saw each other for our official first date a few nights later, for dinner at Arturo's, a landmark Italian restaurant in the Village. Twenty-eight years later, we're still partners in life, love, marriage and music. Surely, we've had our ups and downs, and are always working through the challenges of marriage, as it requires. The fact that he's still a traveling musician doesn't make it easy for either of us. As for me, being a restless spirit, always working and striving, doesn't make it easy either. But the foundation of it all is that we're rooted in the confidence that we have each other's back, and are committed to being together till the end of this life's journey.

After my first marriage, I never thought I would be with anyone again, let alone find a love that I knew would survive. But miraculously, he materialized, out of the blue, just when I wasn't looking.

Our wedding in Woodstock
Photo by Dion Ogust

Childless Mother

"It's a shallow life that doesn't give a person a few scars" - Garrison Keillor

Part of transplanting myself back to New York City was reconnecting with old doctors, finding new ones, and setting up other practical concerns for my life and career. I was re-rooting myself back into the East Coast soil, abandoning the thought of ever going back to Los Angeles.

Since I was turning forty years old, I was already feeling the uptick in menopausal symptoms. The night sweats, irritability, terrible mood swings, and just feeling like my body was running hotter, like the planet with climate change, than my younger self remembered.

I set up an appointment with the last gynecologist I had seen in the early '80s, who was part of a women's doctors group in downtown Manhattan. I gave up on seeing male gynecologists after several difficulties in my twenties. The particular woman doctor I wanted to see wasn't available for some time, so I agreed to meet with one of her colleagues.

I had the usual routine check-up examination, including a pap smear. Since I had had cervical cancer, stage three going into a stage four, when I was twenty-seven years old, I needed to keep up with my routine pap smears every year. Thankfully, with the surgical procedure of a cone biopsy back then, which is basically your cervix being cored like an apple, they were able to get all the cancerous cells out, never to return.

Since I had not gotten pregnant with my first husband, and probably should have, the doctor wanted to do a deeper examination of my uterus with an ultrasound. I remember lying on the table, nonchalantly chatting with the doctor, thinking it was all just part of a routine procedure. A weighty silence abruptly blanketed the air when the doctor asked me, "Have you ever been pregnant?" I explained that I had been pregnant in my late teens and early twenties and had had a couple of abortions.

She proceeded with her questioning and asked, "What happened after that? Were there any other traumatic health events?" I began to describe my horrifying history with IUDs after that. I had a male doctor in New Jersey in those days. He had prescribed at first a Dalcon Shield, which was a popular contraceptive intrauterine device in the 1970s and '80's. I was young and uninformed, so I went along with his advice.

When the Dalcon Shield was first inserted, I remember it being excruciating. The doctor said the pain would subside and my body would get used to it. But the pain never diminished, and I developed a septic infection in my uterus as a result. My body rejected this torturous foreign object. So a D & C (dilation and curettage) was ordered by the doctor, so he could remove the IUD and clean out the infection.

If you research the history of the Dalcon Shield, you see that thousands of women had a similar reaction to the one I had. It caused an array of severe injuries, including pelvic infections, infertility, unintended pregnancies, and even death. I heard recently that someone's wife had died as a result of having one. It was eventually taken off the market and banned by the FDA. But like many medical mistakes like this, it wasn't widely advertised to the public back then that it was a faulty device.

After a few months of healing from the D & C surgical procedure, I went back to the doctor to get on another form of birth control. I didn't want to go on the pill because there were terrible stories about the pill in those days. The doses were much higher, and I didn't like the idea of altering my body chemistry. So the doctor advised me to try another IUD called a Copper Coil.

Since my parents never talked about sex education, or sex period, I was on my own, navigating through all these health issues as a young woman. Therefore, I entrusted the doctor to advise me. I agreed with trepidation to try the Copper Coil. Not surprisingly, my body reacted the same exact way as it did to the Dalcon Shield. I got another pelvic infection and another procedure to remove it and clean out the infection.

Fast forward to being forty years old, I discovered that those experiences with the IUDs damaged my uterus so severely that I could never have gotten pregnant. My uterus was left irreparably scarred and infertile. It was only at that moment on the examination table, that day of my check-up, that I realized I would never be able to have children, as much as I had hoped I could someday. I was devastated.

I probably should have sued the company that made those devices when I discovered the shocking truth about how my reproductive abilities were destroyed. I felt violated and robbed of my biological right as a woman to bear children. And I was psychologically and emotionally shattered. But many years had gone by, and I assumed the statute of limitations had run out. I read that A.H.Robbins, who made the Dalcon Shield, went bankrupt and was later sold to American Home Products. Many women sued and won millions of dollars in claims for damages and medical fees. Other unfortunate women died.

As I look back on this moment in my life, I'm grateful I survived this hideous period of women's health history. But there remains a little bit of sadness that I don't have the pleasure of having grown children now, and possibly grandchildren, to enrich my life and enjoy in my elder years. That said, I know having children isn't the answer to happiness and fulfillment in life. And the tragic fact is, there are so many children in the world who are unloved and uncared for. Regardless, I think I would have loved being a mother.

But the truth be told, I was so career-oriented in those days. And coming out of a bad first marriage, I'm so glad I didn't have children with that man. It would have tied me to him forever. And Danny, being a musician too, was never really interested in having children. Life was challenging enough trying to live as a working artist. Consequently, it worked out for me in that way.

I'm not sure I've really resolved that trauma and loss completely. Instead, I've learned to accept that, for whatever reason, it wasn't meant for me to have my own family. I realized that the inherent womanly instincts and nurturing qualities I possessed needed to be channeled elsewhere. Whether it be through creative pursuits, pets, or towards other people's children, those feelings needed a place to live. Those motherly instincts have never gone away for me. But I've learned to utilize those enshrined nurturing energies differently. I discovered that I could still be a mother of sorts in the world, just not to biological offspring. I would instead be destined to be a childless moth

Running Wild

"You create your thoughts, your thoughts create your intentions, and your intentions create your reality" - Wayne W. Dyer

At this point, Danny and I were living together in an East Village loft that we shared with a friend of his, Rick Robinson. It was a grimy, concrete bachelor pad that I had major issues with, but it was a very spacious and very affordable place for us to join forces as a couple. We had a nice-sized bedroom with almost floor-to-ceiling south-facing windows that made for a cheery, bright space. It makes a significant difference in NYC if you have sunlight in your apartment.

In an adjacent room, I was able to set up my little studio space and office, as well as my Gohanzon. It was a space where I could be quiet, chant, and attend to my personal business. Danny was working at NY Noise full-time then, cranking out jingles for TV and radio. He would leave every day around 10 am, and not get home sometimes until midnight. The company was doing really well at that time, and Danny was winning a notable number of spots. Living in this shared loft apartment allowed him to save a lot of money, which would later go into a down payment on our house upstate.

I, on the other hand, was in a weird kind of limbo at this point. I didn't have a record deal. I didn't want to do club dates and work at local clubs. And soon, the alimony from my divorce was going to run out. That flow of money had been keeping me afloat and gave me a financial and emotional buffer for a few years. But now it was time to put nose to the grindstone and get serious about what my next focus of work was going to be.

I had always been a physically oriented person, all my life. I danced when I was younger. I did ballet, tap, and acrobatics from the age of five to twelve, and thought I wanted to be a dancer. However, being tall and Asian-looking, that dream was quickly dashed by some overly critical teachers. After that, I started running. Or I did yoga. Or was a gym rat. At this point in time, I was running a lot. I ran at least five miles a day, four or five days a week. It helped me stay in shape and deal with anxiety, and it was private time, when I could listen to a lot of music. It was the era of the Walkman, cassette tapes, and wire and foam headsets: nothing fancy, but they got the job done. Music was the bubble my mind could escape to. And it always helped maintain the rhythm of my strides with energy and elation.

This was 1999, and Sting's Brand New Day record had come out in September that year. I had always been a fan of his songwriting, so I bought a cassette of it to accompany me on my runs. Many of the songs had a good tempo and a positive message that gave me an optimistic feeling, especially at a time when I was grappling with what my future would be. Societally, the emerging predictions of a Y2K calamity were swirling round the news and through the heads of humanity, which was also disconcerting.

Every day for months, I cranked out Brand New Day, and with it bleeding through my headphones I ran like a wild horse from our apartment on Second Street to the East River. I streaked parallel to the FDR and circled around a track down by the river. Round and round I would gallop with Sting's music rushing through my veins like a needle shot of caffeine. It could have been any music playing I suppose, but this was prominent on my playlist and priming the pump of my psyche. It wasn't premeditated or conscious. I was just enjoying it.

Mind you, I was chanting every day at this time, since Wayne Shorter and Ana coddled me into their spiritual fold. That spiritual practice inspired radical changes in my life. It literally shifted the ground beneath my feet and altered the state of my reality a hundred and eighty degrees.

So there I was, vigorously running almost every day. Running from the past. Running for answers. Running for change. Chasing desires and dreams with the sounds of Sting's music flooding into the synapses of my brain, and pulsing through my veins. Unbeknownst to me, there was a subconscious, metaphysical metamorphosis being birthed inside me. I don't know how else to explain it. It will sound kind of whoo, whoo, crazy to some of you. But a big change was manifesting in the ether around me.

One very ordinary day, I received an unexpected phone call from Darryl Tookes. Darryl was a successful, well-known session singer in NYC for years. He had recorded with everyone: Michael Jackson, Diana Ross, Quincy Jones, Stevie Wonder. He had recorded on numerous sessions, TV and radio commercials galore. He had done very well. It turned out that he had sung some background vocals on Sting's Brand New Day record. Oh? He was calling to see about my availability for Sting's tour. Apparently, Sting had started his tour in September with three girls from London who were like the girl group En Vogue. He wasn't happy with them and he wanted to make a change. Was I available to go on the road? Crazy!

Darryl and I ended up getting together to work out some of the songs and see how we sounded as a section. Then he was to report back to Sting and the road manager, Billy Francis, to let them know of his choice for a female counterpart. Consequently, Darryl took me up to meet Billy at Trump Tower one day in October. He and Sting were in town for business for a few days. I didn't meet Sting at that meeting. But we were told he wanted to make the changeover in the vocal section by the end of the year.

Not long after that meeting, we flew out to Chicago to see the show, hear the band, and meet Sting and the guys in person. After seeing the show that night, we gathered, except the girls, of course, in the hotel bar. We exchanged pleasantries and checked each other out. It felt like dogs meeting in the park for the first time. But that was it. We got the thumbs up, and the next thing I knew, I had a contract in my hand for the tour.

Our first gig was planned for the new millennium celebration at the NBC studios in NYC, for their big New Year's Eve televised event. Darryl and I had just a few weeks to rehearse on our own, learn all the material, get our look together, make plans to pack and shove off to Europe in January. It all happened in a whirlwind of amazement.

I can't help but think that there was some kind of cosmic connection to my workout sessions, blasting Sting's album into my brain, running wild through the streets of the East Village, while subconsciously setting my intentions toward my next step in life. Propelled by positive energy and passion on a metaphysical level, I believe I unknowingly manifested that gig with Sting. Call it a coincidence. Call it synchronicity. Call it magic. Call it whatever you like. But that's how it manifested. That's how I got that gig. Just like that.

Y2K and the First Sting

"If you ignore the red flags, embrace the heartache to come" - Amanda Mosher

The atmosphere was sizzling with chaos due to the predictions of the imminent collapse of computer systems around the world. Some thought it could end the civilized world as we knew it. A mixed soup of cynicism permeated popular belief in NYC, but a backdrop of fear was undeniable. It was my first gig with Sting, at the NBC Studios for the 1999 New Year's Eve Y2K worldwide broadcast. That was enough for me to concentrate on, never mind a doomsday scenario.

I remember splurging for a cab from my East Village apartment that day and the driver taking me up the east side to avoid midtown traffic. I was left off just near Rockefeller Center, around Fifth Ave and 50th St. It was mid-afternoon, but already police barricades were blocking regular pedestrian and auto traffic from approaching anywhere near the perimeter of Times Square and the Rock. There were heightened security measures set in place around landmarks and government buildings. Widespread fears of computerized security systems going down and possible criminal activities were elevated.

When I confronted the blue police blockade, I found that my name was on a special guest list for the privileged people who were allowed to enter the inner sanctum of Rockefeller Center and the NBC studios. It was always a bit of an ego rush, being let into places where the general public wasn't allowed. But that night, it felt particularly distinguished. I have to say that after many years of "being in the band" and on the road, that privilege became an expected perk of my lifestyle in the high-level rock 'n' roll music business. At that point in my career, I was admittedly a bit jaded.

Soundcheck on the famed Saturday Night Live NBC Studio 8H stage, for Darryl Tookes, the other background singer and me, was a nerve-racking, critical moment. For us, it was the moment to connect with Sting and the band before the ball drop, which would be simultaneous with the downbeat of the song 'Brand New Day'. We were to usher in the new millennium and officially kick off our tour with him. It was the solitary moment to answer any eleventh-hour questions regarding musical arrangements, get our ears attuned to the sonic ambiance of the band, observe the stage set up, and attempt to acclimate ourselves quickly. We were just hours away from promenading ourselves on stage to be scrutinized on camera, singing live in the face of millions of viewers from around the world. It felt like we were preparing to enter a Roman coliseum to battle lions in front of blood-hungry spectators and the Emperor.

Darryl, who had sung on Sting's record, hadn't previously performed live with him. So I think we were both equally nervous coming in to replace the previous background vocalists. It was a lot to take in on such a high-pressure day. The music, the stage, the crew, the politics etc… On top of that, Sting was constantly fiddling about with the music, playing with precision, going over things, seeing how it could be improved upon. Understandably, he was a bit of a perfectionist.

I also found out that it wasn't an uncommon occurrence for him to have whimsical changes of heart with band members, hiring and firing as he saw fit, like moving chess pieces on a board. Good to know. After all, he was a BIG rock star, and it was HIS show.

The soundcheck proceeded without any major hitches. Sting seemed to be pleased with our sound, including the Middle Eastern-styled solo on the song 'Desert Rose' that he assigned to me. Cheb Mami, who sang the original solo on the record, was home in Algeria, and it was an essential piece of the arrangement. It was gratifying to finally sing through all the songs with the band rather than just practicing with the recordings. I felt a little less nervous after getting through the soundcheck, like a horse that has run a few laps around the track, letting off steam before the big race.

After a long "hurry up and wait" dinner break, doing hair and makeup, and transforming myself to be camera-ready, we all arranged ourselves into position on the stage. Breathlessly, we awaited the strike of midnight and the dawn of the new millennium. The band members, Sting, the studio audience, the throngs gathered at Times Square and everyone located across Standard East Coast time anxiously watched and listened for the countdown.

"5-4-3-2-1!" Ball drop! Bang! We were out of the gate, and there was no turning back now.

The band boldly blared out 'Brand New Day': the song for the dawning of a new year, a new age, and the turn of a new century. We were being broadcast on the big screen in Times Square and all over the NBC international network. It was exhilarating! This kind of roller coaster thrill of performing was what hooked me to music and the stage when I was a young girl. After twenty-five years or so living the life of a working professional singer, the excitement of that moment still made my heart soar with elation. It charged my body with a lightning bolt of excitement, like riding the Cyclone at Coney Island or maybe even taking a jolt of cocaine. I had been addicted to that high of the stage and bright lights for a long time, and it hadn't lost its luster.

After 'Brand New Day', only a few other songs in the set were slated to be part of the worldwide broadcast. NBC had more entertainment scheduled, so the rest of Sting's show continued for the few hundred private party guests who were in the audience at Studio 8H. Danny, my boyfriend, who later became my husband, was there, and my old friends Elizabeth Oei and Adrienne Pappas had flown in from Los Angeles to be there as well. It was an especially celebratory night, and it turned out that the new millennial world was still spinning around us as usual. The computer bug of Y2K barely left a scratch. It was more like a joke than a horror.

Later, backstage in the hospitality suite, bubbling jubilance clinked and clanked amongst illustrious guests, friends, and family of the band. Expensive champagne was flowing, and exotic hors d'oeuvres were plentiful. Darryl and I were showered with adulation from the band and management. And a flow of satisfaction filled us from achieving a job well done. We had jumped head-first into the deep end of a pool without life preservers and had successfully stayed afloat.

At one point, in the witching hour of the evening, Sting came over to where I was enjoying the company of my friends. He made general small talk about the momentous event of the evening. Meantime, as recounted by my friend Elizabeth, various people were coming up to me, complimenting me on my solo in 'Desert Rose'.

"Great job!"

"You sounded amazing!"

"What an amazing voice!"

I repeatedly replied, "Thank you so much" to everyone who came up to me, for their kind words. It was overwhelming.

Sting watched and listened attentively. I thought he might be pleased with my debut performance. But I sensed discomfort on his face. I couldn't quite put my finger on it. Nor could I imagine why he might be displeased. Then, in a surprisingly awkward moment, he looked toward me, with my friends as my witnesses… he paused… and said:

"That was really good… maybe a little too good."

Then walked away.

With Sting on Y2k New Years Eve 1999/2000
at NBC Studio H

The Second Sting: Beginning the End

"Fool me once, shame on you; fool me twice, shame on me" - Anthony Weldon 1651 based on an Italian proverb

Most of the Sting tour following the Y2K New Year's show was focused on Europe. We played many typical venues we used to call "sheds". They were mostly old sporting arenas that had been converted into concert halls. These venues were never intended to be acoustically friendly to loud, electric music, so you can imagine how the sound environments were usually reflective, reverberating boxes of ricocheting noise. But they were large spaces that could hold thousands of people and support large box office ticket sales for acts like Sting and Foreigner, with whom I remember doing some similar venues in the 80s.

For me and Darryl, the European leg of the tour started in France at the Zenith in Lille. We did a number of shows in various towns in France, where Sting is clearly beloved, as he is almost everywhere. We did a one-off show in Milan, Italy. Then back to a few more shows in France. From there, we moved on to a furious succession of shows in Germany, Denmark, Switzerland, the Czech Republic, Sweden, Finland, Poland, Slovakia, Belgium, Holland and finally Ireland and the UK. It was a magical ending in the UK with nine shows in a row at the elegant and prestigious Royal Albert Hall.

These months of touring in January through March were kind of bleak. It was winter. It was mostly chilly, damp, and gray, which gives everything a muted, Game of Thrones kind of tone. Old and musty, yet seductively charming. It's impossible to not be captivated by the beautiful architecture and rich history. I've always loved traveling in Europe, taking in the picturesque sites, the food, and the delicious wine wherever I go. I've always felt at home in Europe. England has a magnetic pull for me with family history and my last name being Taylor. I have ancestral roots there from my father's side of the family. That said, I've always been particularly attracted to Italy. Perhaps it's because of some Italian heritage somewhere along the bloodline. More likely, it's my love of how the Italians are so expressive, how they fiercely hold family dear, and how they seem to simply enjoy life in a way that I adore and have always desired. Their lifestyle is the absolute opposite of what I grew up with.

Nevertheless, all that culture, food, and wine never make up for home and the place where your heartstrings are tethered. I was missing home like I had never done before in all my years of touring. Danny and I had recently become a couple, just six months earlier, and I missed him terribly. To combat the loneliness, I hung out a lot and was drinking more… more than usual. I took to partying with the tour manager, the band, the crew, and whoever from the tour was lingering about after the shows. I just didn't want to go to my room and be alone. No matter how posh and beautiful a five-star hotel room can be, it can still be a chamber of aching emptiness at night. The dramatic shift from the exalted atmosphere of being in front of thousands of screaming fans, gearing down to just being by yourself, can be disturbing. It's like bungee jumping off a beautiful scenic cliff over the ocean, thinking you're going for a joy ride, only to find the cable snap, plunging you to the water below. You need to know how to swim. I think for anyone who hasn't experienced road life, this is the most challenging part of that lifestyle, and the least understood by outsiders.

I don't know why, but I have to say that I'm flashing on Anthony Bourdain right now. I was a big fan. How depressed and lonely he must have felt when he killed himself in his hotel room in France a few years ago. It breaks my heart to think about what his last night of life must have been like. I'm not saying that I was ever that depressed or felt suicidal. But I can imagine that kind of loneliness and sinking into a deep, dark place of despair. I hope you're at peace now Tony.

I know it's hard for most people who aren't in the entertainment business to truly understand what it's like to be on the road on a big tour. Most of the time is spent shuffling around, traveling, and dragging your belongings behind you like a nomadic tribesman. You're either on a plane or on a tour bus, to-ing and fro-ing from city to city, country to country, and stage to stage. There are only a few hours of the day that you're actually doing the show. Most of the time is in-between downtime and life in limbo. It's not at all the glamor and glitter that it appears to be from afar. It's the life of a salesman, a circus carny, and a vagabond rolled into one. Even though the accommodations and food are pretty nice, you're still roaming around the earth with your luggage, showing your wares. Of course, if you're a mega star, the experience is quite different, and you're most likely surrounded by people all the time. But nevertheless, it's a circus.

It takes a tremendous sense of drive to want to be a "star" and endure the grueling schedules and unsettled life one must exist with, to live in the limelight. Though I was never a center-stage star, I lived in the shadows of enough of them. It was never a life I desired. Yes, of course, the success and money would've been nice. But the sacrifice of privacy, anonymity, and normalcy, along with the loss of freedom to move about the world as one wishes, never seemed appealing. It honestly seemed like a cumbersome burden. A kind of prison, if you will.

That said, having worked with some stars, I was a peripheral benefactor of their grandiose lifestyles while on tour. And Sting was certainly in the upper echelon of that world then. Private jets, five-star hotels, first-class everything, and that world behind the velvet rope, the inner sanctum of stardom. For better or worse, I'll forever be grateful for those experiences. I'm incredibly lucky to have had such prodigious memories to stash in my memory banks for a lifetime or more.

Getting back to the European leg of Sting's tour, I recall that one night we were in Rotterdam doing a show in a particularly loud, tin-can arena. Sting wasn't feeling well that night, and it was evident in his voice during the show. It wasn't bad, but he just wasn't his best self. We were doing the show as usual, and it came time for me to do the solo on 'Desert Rose', which I had been doing every night. All night, there was this awful slap-back of sound from the room, and particularly from this center-hanging scoreboard not far away from the stage. It was grating and cacophonous. It wasn't a pleasant sound or experience for any of us. As I started singing my solo, I remember hearing it come back to me in almost an embarrassing way. It was loud and up front, so there was no hiding it. But the audience was going crazy, loving it. I got a huge round of applause. I thought I'd had a good show.

The following day, Bill Francis, the tour manager, said he needed to speak with me. So Daryl and I met with him before the soundcheck. Bill said that the "boss" didn't want me to do the solo in 'Desert Rose' any more because it sounded too Oriental. At first, I laughed, because, in its musical essence, the solo was basically Oriental, since Cheb Mami, who sang the original on the record, was Algerian. But Billy's tone of voice and use of that derogatory term sharply delivered his point. I understood what he alluded to was serious and wasn't a joke. The truth was that I was being relegated to stay in my musical place in the background, and out of the way of the boss's limelight. I had clearly infringed upon his space, especially during the show the night before when he wasn't feeling well. At that moment, I felt slapped in the face with the truth that being 20 Feet from Stardom is to know your place.

I felt beaten down and angry. I knew that I had been killing the solo every night, but I was clearly being punished because of it. It seemed evident to me that Sting felt threatened, which shocked me. And that's not conjecture or a self-aggrandizing thought. I was already aware that Sting didn't like it when Chris Botti held out the ending note on the song 'Bourbon Street' longer than he did, which seemed shallow. I became cognizant of the fact that even with all that star power, success, and money, Sting wasn't immune to human frailty. It was an awakening. It changed my whole perspective about him and about people in his position.

At that point, I thought about going home. I was livid. But I was tormented because I needed the work and the money, which was substantial. Part of me didn't want to put up with the ego-fueled politics that were circling around me. And I missed Danny terribly. I would have preferred being home with him. But I stayed and decided to tough it out, even though the enthusiasm and creative enjoyment of the gig got gut-punched out of me.

There is a saying that one should never meet one's idols. Now I understand why.

The Sting Operation

"When we least expect it, life sets us a challenge to test our courage and willingness to change" - Paulo Coelho

I had only been touring with Sting since the beginning of the year, but it felt arduously longer. The weightiness of the atmosphere around the situation never felt completely comfortable to me from day one. After a few challenging moments along the way and my 'Desert Rose' solo execution, the air felt thick with a palpable sense of unease. It was like perceiving the electromagnetic change in the atmospheric pressure before an earthquake. Like an animalistic instinct, it felt primitive. I imagine that sense aligns with the illusory, rarified air of the inner sanctum orbit with celebrities and the rich and powerful. There has to be a lot of tension to sustain that kind of high-wire walking kind of life.

    I had the feeling that one had to walk on eggshells around Sting. That you had to be careful not to upset the powers that be, whoever they might be. There were many people to beware of, whether it was Sting himself, his wife Trudy, the manager - who at the time was Miles Copeland, the tour manager, or even certain band members who might betray you. It was a world of covert activity. It was a big tent circus, and this was a high-wire act. The background singers were just a balancing tool for the star funambulist. We were commoners in the land of royalty. Hail the king, or he might have your head.

    Daryl Tookes and I had dinner in the hotel restaurant in New Orleans, the night before the New Orleans Jazz Festival show. We were both feeling pretty worn out from the whirlwind of the last several months. I recall that he was feeling strangely uncertain about our professional fate. He sensed something odd, but couldn't put his finger on it. He said something to the effect of, "I think something is up and we might get fired." There had undoubtedly been a few red flags waved recently, but I thought there was nothing that would put us in jeopardy of losing our gigs. It was normal to have some tense moments on any tour. Spending so much time intimately traveling with people you hardly know is unnatural. And then to share that intimate experience of playing music together on stage in front of thousands of people? It's uniquely bizarre and wonderful all at once. Regardless, I was a bit shocked about Daryl's premonition, which made me feel dreadfully uneasy. So I tried to take the high road and a more optimistic route. I deflected his voice of doom and plugged up my ears with denial. I proclaimed how I felt we were doing a great job, and why we shouldn't worry. Why would there be any reason for Sting not to be happy with us?

As we walked out of the restaurant, I noticed Sting and several others in a private booth with an unknown person. I didn't stop to say hello, respecting their privacy. It was dark and it didn't appear that they had seen us. So we walked out.

Show day in the dressing room trailer at the New Orleans Jazz Festival was, in hindsight, an ominous day. It wasn't the normal posh dressing room setup, as it never is with these humongous multi-act festivals, set up in football stadium-sized outdoor fields. The trailer was bare, except for a few coolers jammed with a variety of drinks. Some round plastic trays of cheap deli crudités were strewn along the counters. I do remember the horrible fluorescent lighting with that sick, yellowish glow and the trailer park trash linoleum floors. More significantly, I can summon the eerie sense that the band members were averting their eyes from me. The air felt muddy and dense, hovering above the usual, musky New Orleans humidity. People were oddly quiet. I just thought everyone was tired or hungover and looking forward to the little break that was about to begin the following day.

The show came off without a hitch, as expected. It was nothing unusual for that caliber of musicians and stage crew. Sting was the headliner that night on the big Acura stage. The hyperbolic enthusiasm from the crowd when we finished made you feel like you were walking on water. It was the "Big Rock Show" after all. The endorphins were rushing as usual. I walked off the stage with a feeling of all-is-right-with-the-world. As if we had landed an impeccable gymnastic flip with graceful precision. My naive state of bliss would soon be shattered, with Peter Gabriel's song 'Big Time' poignantly playing in the background.

The next day, at the airport, a few of us were traveling to NYC on the same plane. Others had different flights back to London, Paris, and other destinations. Daryl and I were walking to our gate, but decided to stop and call his answering machine at home. (Strange to think this was before cell phones were common.) I was standing next to him while he was listening to his messages. I suddenly noticed his look of utter shock, and his handsome African-American face draining pale.

"What's wrong?"

"You're not going to believe this."

"What?"

"We've been let go."

"What do you mean?"

"Miles Copeland left me a message saying our services will no longer be needed."

Shockingly, Daryl's suspicions were prophetic.

I was paralyzed. My body flooded with a hot, fiery rush, like a tiny napalm bomb going off inside my chest. My mind was in complete disbelief, as if I were watching a bizarre episode of The Twilight Zone. Or smoking some over-amped weed. I became an unemployed zombie in the blink of an eye.

First of all, who fires someone by leaving a message on an answering machine? It's cowardly and cold. It's the equivalent of breaking up with someone through a text message these days. It's so lame. But Miles never gave me a warm and fuzzy feeling. Secondly, why didn't Sting, the tour manager, or anyone else speak to us face-to-face first, out of respect or kindness? Really? Never before had I been treated with such heartless disregard. Never before had I been let go from a job. Ever! This was emotional territory I was completely unfamiliar with. It was as foreign as walking on the Alaskan tundra or the moon. I was numb.

At that moment, I remember starting to cry from the sheer shock. Then, in a panic, I decided I needed an answer. I quickly ran to find the departure gate of the keyboard player, Kipper, who I thought of as a friend. Maybe he could let me in on the secret as to what happened. I did find Kipper. He apologized and said that he did go to bat for us and that it wasn't anything personal. It was more of a conceptual idea for Sting. He wanted the band to have more of a rock 'n' roll edge. Whatever that meant. The rest is a blur.

We boarded the plane to NYC, and I was a whimpering mess. I felt so hurt and devastated. How could Sting not be happy with me? And furthermore, how could he not have the decency to tell me to my face? I think I cried the whole way back to NYC and mumbled, "I can't believe it."

That moment ripped the scab off old, forgotten wounds, triggering painful childhood emotions of being torn away from my grandmother and my birth land with no explanation. It activated deep-rooted feelings of abandonment and fathomless sadness. It surfaced ghostly images of ancient disappointments right down to ancestral trauma. And it reenacted the wrongs of the most consequential people in my life. My parents.

I wasn't conscious of the violent quake of subconscious terrain awakening within me then. Nor was I equipped to deal with it. It was a massive tectonic psychic shift that took down the scaffolding of my persona, stripping me bare. I was broken once again, but in a novel way. A million pieces of myself scattered into the abyss. An existential crisis.

On the surface of reality and in the eyes of others, it was just a professional drama that happens all the time in business. Differing visions and inharmonious chemistry. But I had never encountered anything like this. Nothing personal? It was like a direct stab into my heart. Not just a surface wound. For me, it was deeply personal.

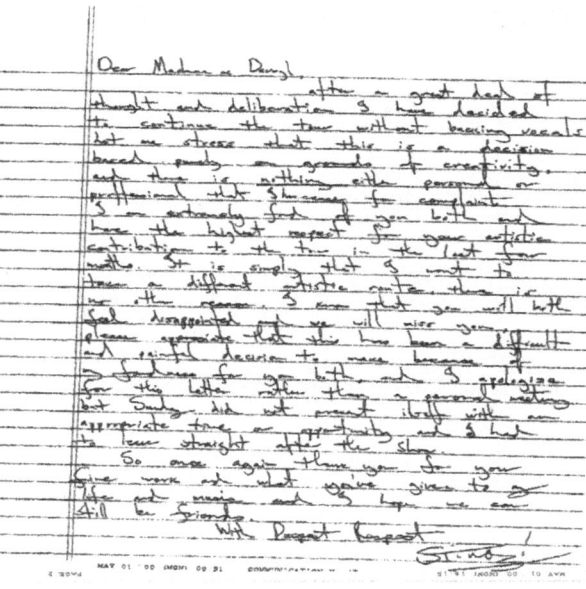

Roxanne Music

FAX COVER SHEET   May 4, 2000

FROM: William Francis
TO: Machan & Darryl
COMPANY: N/A
REGARDING: Things
FAX NO: 212 925 4798

NUMBER OF PAGES INCLUDING THIS ONE (1) IF TRANSMISSION IS INCOMPLETE PLEASE CALL THE ABOVE NUMBERS

Dear Machan and Darryl,

This is the fourth time I've tried to write this letter, whatever way I try to explain to you and myself how and why this happened it all sounds so contrite, I agree with most of your complaints and I'm very sad it ended in this manner.

Sometimes the boss makes decisions which we do not understand, this is one on those times and I'm very sorry this has caused you so much pain and anguish.

I will make sure you get all your personal items from the wardrobe case, I will also expedite your severance payment as per contract, to enable this to happen please send your remaining airline tickets to Miriam Murphy at Phillips & Gold, the address is in the old itinerary.

I wish you well for the future and hope you have some good thoughts on the time spent with us, please take care and good luck.

Kind Regards

William Francis

After the Rain Has Fallen

"You don't learn from successes; you don't learn from awards; you don't learn from celebrity; you only learn from wounds and scars and mistakes and failures. And that's the truth" - Jane Fonda

Back home in NYC, I was inconsolable. Danny couldn't understand why I was so upset. He just thought that a gig is just a gig, shit happens, and you move on to the next thing. He was able to be objective in a way that I wasn't. I was taking on the situation way too seriously.

It's never easy to see the whole picture when you're focused on one small aspect of it. It's like standing with your face smack dab in front of a masterly painting, instead of from a distance. You can't possibly absorb the whole visual experience of what the artist intended. I wasn't ready in that moment to see the situation for what it was... just another bump in the road.

It was hard for me to "just move on." So I wallowed in self-pity, longer than I maybe should have. But surprisingly, wallowing was how I could sit still long enough to find the nuggets of gold that paved the way to peace. In Buddhism, they say, "Don't just do something, sit there." So I did.

In hindsight, I now understand why I took losing the Sting gig so badly. It wasn't just the humiliating fact that Sting never confronted Daryl and me directly while the band knew what was going on. Or the insensitive and inconsiderate way of letting us go via a voice message from management.

I realized that why it felt like such a blow was because the situation drilled down into the interconnection of one of my core emotional issues. It hit a nerve that was so deeply linked to those old childhood scars. And a pattern of me giving my power away to powerful men in my life. It was the ghosts of my father and my family. It triggered me to feel like it was my fault. I was to blame for my father being an alcoholic, a gambler, and a womanizer. I was the reason my mother was so unhappy. It was because of me that we left Japan and I never saw my grandmother again. And I was the reason Sting decided to change the band's personnel. It was my fault because I WASN'T GOOD ENOUGH.

Really, Machan? Nail on the head! Bingo! History repeating.

There it was. That deep, nagging, open lesion of trauma that I had been lugging around with me all my life. And here was the perfect storm scenario that stirred up that overly sensitive soup of emotions, allowing me to taste it differently. It was jolting and knocked me over the head. Seeing that shadowy place in myself and bringing it to light was a powerful realization. I was ready to see it for what it was.

Of course, it wasn't my fault. None of it was my fault. However, my emotional reaction to those old scars was my responsibility, even though it stung (pun intended :)). It was debilitating. I knew I had to face the dissonance screaming inside me, but I knew it wouldn't be easy.

Truth be told, I know on a deep level that every difficult experience in my life has been an instructional gift. The revelations that ensued from my challenging childhood, losing my father in my twenties, having cancer in my twenties, the dissolution of my first marriage, losing the Sting gig, etc, were all incredibly beneficent offerings from the universe, guiding me to wisdom and growth. Life paid me a huge favor, giving me new building blocks for my character, and a deepening that my soul longed for. Of course, I didn't appreciate all this at the time. Wisdom only comes from going through the process, time, and reflection. We all have to pay our dues to claim the rewards.

Beyond all the emotional amelioration that occurred for me, I knew on an intellectual level that there wouldn't be another tour in my future because I didn't want one. I was done. I no longer wanted to do that work or have that life. At that point, I had worked for well over twenty-five years as a touring, working singer and performer. From clubs as a teenager to touring in my twenties and beyond, I had been there and done that. I was ready for change, and this situation forced its hand.

So I began letting go, and mourning the death of an old definition of me. The release of ideals and dreams that I had lived out. These aspects of myself were so ingrained that they no longer felt fresh or inspiring. Being a background singer at that level had been great work. It was a musical success and professional success. But it wasn't artistically fulfilling or satisfying anymore. It was an adolescent dream fulfilled. As the title of the movie 20 Feet from Stardom aptly expressed, you're standing in the shadows. You're not the main artist, the star, the bandleader, or in the spotlight. You're a side person. And in several cases, it was working with challenging politics or under the thumb of a man. Perhaps that's just life. But I ended up feeling like an old milk horse traveling a well-worn path. I could do it in my sleep, which is not an exhilarating way to live. It was time for a growth-seeking shift within myself.

In hindsight many years later, losing that gig with Sting was one of the best things that could have happened to me. It was a bitch slap from God, a wake-up call from the universe. It motivated me to transform in countless ways. So for that, I'm beholden. For some reason, we humans don't always naturally initiate change unless we've been brought to the brink of bottoming out in a state of misery. Or to the point where we can no longer live in denial. We get comfortably complacent, or shall I say comfortably numb, to a certain state of being. Like staying in a bad relationship, even when we know it's over.

I was being kicked out of my comfort zone, like a fledgling leaving the nest. I needed to learn how to fly on my own. I was entering into the realm of the teachings of Don Juan. I was stepping into the desert and uncharted territory. I would need to be an apprentice for a while before the teacher would accept me. I would need to walk through the fire to burn off the delusions that had been keeping me blind to myself and blocked from what I needed to know. There would be many trials along the way and a new added dimension to my future self.

The Birth of a New Dream

"Our need will be the real creator" - Plato

When I arrived home from the Sting tour in May 2000, a nationwide Screen Actors Guild strike unraveled. It would turn out to be the longest-running union strike in Hollywood history. A strike meant that no one in the SAG union could work. Point blank.

If you know anything about the jingle business back then, recording sessions and TV commercials for singers paid very well. It was a great way to make money. It was a full-time career for many musicians and singers, but also great part-time work for people like me while in town off the road. Even though the actual glory days of the jingle business were long gone, you could, if you were lucky, get a few major commercials and make enough money to live on for a year or more. But you had to do union jobs to make those kinds of residuals. I was dead in the water.

To make matters worse, Danny had been making his money writing jingles at that point, before he joined Gov't Mule. He had just won a huge Kentucky Fried Chicken campaign. He was set to make almost a cool quarter of a million dollars. Unfortunately, because he was in the union and NY Noise was a signatory union house, they were forbidden from recording the final production of that music. It would have been aired on prime-time TV with major rotation for a long run. I had also sung on the campaign demos, meaning I would've been on the final commercial too. Now, all bets were off. Scab workers recorded the broadcast versions, and we were all damned out of luck.

The strike painfully dragged on from May to October that year. And though I had some money in the bank, I needed to work and figure out new ways to make money. What would I do after being left shell-shocked by Sting? Ha! Say that ten times fast.

At a loss for any immediate ingenious ideas, I did what many out-of-work artists in NYC typically do. I decided to take a waitressing job at a well-known health food restaurant near our apartment called Spring Street Natural. I hadn't waitressed in eons, but I thought getting out of the house and being with people would be good for me. I hadn't anticipated that taking that job would be such a major psychic blow. But when I put on the company apron and orthotic working shoes, I felt like I had fallen into a black hole of non-existence. It prompted visions of one of those falling-down-out-of-the-sky dreams that everyone seems to have in times of stress. But it felt like I wasn't going to wake up. I was endlessly falling, descending from the heights of performing at places like the Grammys and the Royal Albert Hall, to a nowhere Greenwich Village health food restaurant, serving coffee and sandwiches. (At least the food was organic.)

I barely made a hundred dollars a day, a tiny fraction of what I was used to making on the road. I was a long way from the bright lights and adulations of audiences. It felt like clawing through a dark tunnel with no inkling of salvation in the distance.

Mind you, waitering is a respectable profession. I respect professional service people who are great at their jobs, love to connect with people, and take pride in their work. Living in NYC and going out to eat a lot over the years, there is nothing that makes for a great dining experience more than a high-quality wait person. I'm sincere about that. But I wasn't a good waitress, and it didn't make me happy. Cooking, on the other hand, would have been much more interesting to me. But it's hard work, and it was too late for me to consider being a chef as a career.

After a short, agonizing stint at waitressing, I decided to heed the call of another idea that had been bubbling on the back burner of my brain for some time. Teaching. Teaching voice, perhaps. Hmmm…

I had a history of studying with great teachers when I was a teenager. And I certainly had a lot of experience as a professional singer by then. But I wasn't sure I had the skill to put it all together and actually impart what I knew in a palatable way to students. The only way to find out was to do it.

To get started, I decided to take a small ad out in the Village Voice newspaper, which everyone at the time referred to for all kinds of services (there was no Instagram or Facebook then), from seeking sexual encounters to selling used home goods, musical instruments, and, of course, lessons for whatever you could think of. New York City was still a mecca for up-and-coming performers, so I figured I might attract at least a few students to begin my teaching odyssey.

After the ad in the Village Voice came out, I swiftly and surprisingly started getting calls from students wanting lessons. They came to my apartment, which at that point was a spacious loft on Mulberry St. It was a comfortable environment to invite people into. I had an electric piano in my little production studio, which was enough to get me started.

Feeling like a newborn foal at first, it took me a little while to get my footing and build my confidence. But I had studied enough to understand the format of lessons, vocal technique, methodology, and presentation. And I understood singers because I was one. I understood the care needed to work with their ego sensitivities and sense of vulnerability.

The voice is an instrument directly connected to a person's body, emotions, and self-expression. It's personal. There is no hiding with the voice. And as the vocal physiological construct of every human being is unique, so is the quality of their instrument, the character of their sound, and the physical structure housing it. I think it's a magnificent and unique part of who we are as human creatures.

During those early teaching ventures in my apartment, there was a gravity to the experience that cracked open a new, illuminated place inside me. It was an unfamiliar joy with a rich, lasting essence unlike anything else I'd known to that point. It was fresh and inspiring. It was my AHA! moment.

I discovered that teaching and paying forward my knowledge and experience was something I was good at and felt incredibly comfortable with. I loved caring for other people and their vocal and musical needs. Being of service made me feel good. Perhaps my dysfunctional family setup oddly equipped me to be inclined to be a good caretaker. It's part of my nature. In the context of teaching, it was a beneficial skill and an appropriate perk.

The lessons I had invested in for myself for years were paying off. And my well-seasoned life experience was leading me to something greater than I could imagine. Music once again piloted me to a new frontier, a new purpose, and a new vocation. I didn't know it then, but it chaperoned me through the looking glass to an undiscovered realm of myself, and a new dimension to my life.

The Day Everything Changed

"Life changes in the instant. The ordinary instant" - Joan Didion

It was a beautifully clear September day. The sky was a shimmery blue, and the air smelled so clean and fresh for New York City. It just felt like a "life is good" t-shirt kind of day. I had already been up and out with my dog Luna early in the morning, and I was back inside, feeding him and having my morning coffee.

At about 8:55am, my friend John Pace called and said, "Turn on your TV, you won't believe what's happened." As I began to watch the news and heard the report of a plane that had just hit the World Trade Center North, I couldn't believe what a horrible accident this was. Not long after, another jet hit the south tower, and we all knew it wasn't an accident. It was something more sinister, and more horrifying, than we could fathom. We were under attack and possibly at war.

I immediately called Danny, who was away rehearsing with Gregg Allman in Georgia, getting ready for a tour. When he picked up the phone, he was still asleep. In a bit of a panic, I alerted him to what was happening and told him to turn on the news. We said we would speak once he had woken up and had some coffee. Shortly after that, all the phone systems went down. I had no reception. No way to communicate with anyone. Danny and I not being able to reach each other felt incredibly distressing. But I knew that somehow, I'd be ok.

After the reports of the second plane crashing into the towers was confirmed, I decided to go out with Luna and have a look. Since we lived in Little Italy, near the corner of Canal and Center

Street, I walked over there to where I had a clear view of the World Trade Center. Smoke was rapidly billowing out from both towers, filling the sky with a thick layer of acrid air, choking the feel-good feeling I had started the day with into a panic-stricken gasp of absolute disbelief and terror.

People had gathered all around me, mesmerized, staring at the towers on fire, all of us seemingly frozen with the same sense of dread that was rushing through my body. It was as if we were entranced by the spell of a satanic overlord: mouths gaping, eyes transfixed, and dumbfounded by what we were witnessing. It was surreal, but very real at the same time. We were speechless; helpless.

After standing transfixed and immobilized for some time, I noticed people approaching from the downtown area walking toward us. They were covered in ghostly suits of ash and dust, like zombies. They looked shell-shocked. It was clear these people had been in the area of the World Trade Center when the planes hit and got caught in the rain of wreckage fallout. It added another ominous overlap to the feeling that we were participating in some kind of Hollywood horror movie.

I must have stood in a stupor in the same spot for about an hour. According to the internet and the Miller Center website, the South Tower of the World Trade Center collapsed at 9:59 am. I remember the shock of watching this seemingly serene vision of the smoke spewing out of these behemoth buildings and suddenly witnessing a massive movement. Like my childhood memories of atomic bomb blast photos, a mushroom cloud of smoke gracefully ballooned up in the sky above the space where the towers stood. The building simply vanished out of view, like a curtain falling away from the reveal of a new art sculpture or a flip of a magic trick. There was no sound from where I stood. No direct experience of the disintegration. Just the simple agonizing slow motion falling of the South Tower, vaporizing into a cloud; into a memory. Gone. History.

There were gasps and moans all around me. An ensemble cry of "Oh my God" in dissonant harmony. I felt like I couldn't breathe because my body was petrified. The only sense of comfort was clinging to my little five-pound ball of doggie fluff, who had saved my heart several times before.

About a half hour or so later, the North Tower of the World Trade Center collapsed into a similar mushroom puff of obscurity, surrendering itself along with its twin. The World Trade Center was gone as we knew it. Life as we knew it would never return. And the future of the world was a question mark cloud in the sky.

I snapped myself out of the standing stupor and decided to take my dog home and see if I could reach Danny again. No signal. Neither could I reach my friend John, or anyone else I knew. So I decided I needed to do something, and see if I could learn more about what was going on and how I might possibly help.

In an act of desperation, I proceeded walking from Mulberry St in Little Italy, across into SoHo on West Broadway, and up to the Village. It felt like chaos everywhere. Sirens were going off. Ambulances rushing through the streets. Military vehicles were appearing out of nowhere. Otherwise, there were no regular traffic jams, horns honking, and very few people below Houston St. There was a clear and present sense of danger around me. And I felt a crazy mix of heightened anxiety and excitement for the adventure. It felt like I had entered an episode of MASH.

I thought St. Vincent's Hospital on 6th Ave would be a good place to do something positive and maybe donate blood. Surely there would be thousands of victims from the rubble of the tower that would need triage? When I arrived, hundreds of people were already in line to donate blood. After a while of mindless waiting in line, the hospital personnel came out with a bullhorn and announced that they had run out of blood bags and were encouraging us to travel to the Red Cross uptown. A bus was appointed to take us to the Upper West Side, where the Red Cross headquarters was. I found myself shuffling off with a platoon of hypnotized do-gooders, united in wanting to feel like we were doing something, anything, other than being stranded and paralyzed in our fear.

Arriving uptown, the feeling was oddly calm. It was as if upper Manhattan was unaffected by this ghastly drama unfolding downtown. How could that be? It was a weird juxtaposition, deepening the sense of a surrealistic nightmare in broad daylight.

The Red Cross building was bustling. More and more people were arriving with the same mission in mind: donating blood. It's strange to think that in times of need, when you don't possess life-saving skills, the one thing you always have is your own bodily fluid-life-saving blood. When I stumbled off the bus, mumblings of disappointment traveled quickly through the crowd. They too, had run out of blood collection bags, and we were turned away again. Now what?

I was afraid to get on the subway, not knowing what might be going on underground. So I decided to walk back to my apartment downtown. It was a long way, but I needed to be in the fresh air and get a sense of what was happening around the city. I noticed a lot of people congregating in restaurants and bars that were open. I think everyone was looking for solace and community. When I got back to Houston Street, there was a blockade, with police barricading every street that led further south. They were checking IDs and asking questions. Luckily, I had my bag and driver's license with me so I could prove I lived on Mulberry St. They passed me through.

When I got back, my dog was beautifully oblivious to what was going on and he was just so happy to see me. Pets are such a sweet, grounding presence in one's life. I tried the phone again, and the service had been restored. I was finally able to reach Danny. He was already planning to drive back to New York with a few of the guys since all air travel was suspended and the tour was canceled. It would take him a few days, but he reassured me he was on his way.

Late that afternoon, my friend John, who lived on Gold Street near the World Trade Center, made his way to my apartment. He had been stuck in the thick of the stench and dust that was hovering around the Trade Center area and desperately needed to get away.

We went across the street to one of the few restaurants open and decided to eat Italian food and drink some wine. Actually, a lot of wine. We needed to numb out a little to the unexplainable madness of the world. I was so grateful to have the companionship of a friend in that moment.

I remember the restaurant had a TV going with the continuous news coverage of the scenario of the day still unfolding. Shaky video shots of the rubble downtown. Traumatized people running through the streets. Then breaking news flash, President George Bush Jr appeared on the TV screen to address the country. Our fearless leader looked like a bug-eyed deer in the headlights. His blank stare into the camera gave no semblance of confidence and authority. It seemed clear that he was not in charge of himself or of this catastrophe. John and I looked at each other, clanked our glasses together, and toasted, "We're fucked."

Out of the Rubble

"If your world doesn't allow you to dream, move to one where you can" – Billy Idol

The aftermath of 9/11 changed NYC immeasurably. There was a mass exodus of residents and businesses out of the city like I hadn't seen before. The World Trade Center fire pit was still burning for months. We could smell the caustic smoldering ashes in the rubble that you knew included the bodies of those thousands of unfortunate souls who couldn't make it out of the building. It was a dismal and acerbic reminder of the disaster and a health hazard concern for those of us living downtown. Meanwhile, Christine Todd Whitman and the EPA were telling everyone not to worry. We know now that our downplayed fears were actually warranted.

As the world moved on, there was this sense of fear about what the future might bring due to the attacks. But interestingly, on the other end of the spectrum, there was this incredible sense of unity and brotherly love that wrapped its proverbial arms around us New Yorkers and America at large. It was strange, pleasant, and palpable. It was a wonderful sentiment. But it didn't last.

Unfortunately, with so many businesses down and the world in a state of shock, the jingle business and advertising plummeted. Danny's successful run writing commercials for New York Noise saw the end of its joy ride, along with many other companies in the same field. This post-tragic period would birth a new chapter of Danny's professional life, with the joining of Gov't Mule as a member. By 2002, the deal was sealed.

I was still out of work, except for a handful of students. But by 2003, I had acquired my first solo record deal and was working on my first solo record. It was a vision of hope. I was still somewhat rudderless, but I was exploring creative endeavors, writing songs like crazy, and moving into new, artful territory. Danny, as always, was very supportive, allowing me to flounder and probe into a new sphere of being.

With the commercial downturn in NYC, Danny and I started investigating moving out of town and cutting back financially, leaving our overpriced loft for a more sensible dwelling with some property in the country, which we could call home.

By 2004, we had finalized our chapter as Manhattanites and transported a truckload of belongings and our urban lifestyle to the greener pastures of rural Hudson Valley, New York. We had found a wonderful cedar-sided house in a remote area with a nice piece of land, woods, fresh air, fresh water, and a new start. I dug my heels in emotionally as we left the city, but at that point, it didn't make sense to stay. New York had changed. And buying in the city was astronomically expensive. So, holding my breath, I jumped into the deep end of the dirt in the Catskill Mountains.

We moved on Labor Day weekend of 2004, while the weather was still warm and sweet. The fresh country air in the woods was an exhilarating change from the carbon monoxide-laden air of Manhattan. Part of me didn't want to like it, but I did. After only a few days in our new house, Danny had to leave on tour with Gov't Mule for almost a month. And I was left with our little dog, Luna, to unpack, get settled, and figure out the lay of the land.

The first night alone in the house after Danny left was hot and humid. The bedroom didn't have an air conditioner. The windows were wide open as I lay sprawled out on the bed like a starfish, without any cover, oppressed by the weight of the heat, sweating, and restless. As I listened to the cricks and chirps of the night, I suddenly heard the sound of piercing howling. At first, I thought it might be a neighbor's dog down the road. But I quickly realized it came from down the hill in our woods. The sound of a singular howl promptly began to crescendo into a chorus of multiple barks, shrill and loud. Growing up in a very suburban neighborhood in New Jersey, I had no reference for these frightening frequencies echoing through the thick of the night. I panicked! Did we have wolves in our backyard? Were they coming to get me? Could they break into the house?

I jumped out of bed and proceeded to close all the windows, and ran around making sure all the doors were locked. Not only did I think we had a pack of wolves nearby, I remembered there was a state prison not too far away. So maybe there was an escaped convict running around out there too! OMG!! My mind was racing with images of every horror movie I've ever seen, and I swore that I was the next victim in a Freddie Krueger film.

My heart was bouncing on a trampoline out of my chest. I locked myself in the bedroom and prayed to make it safely through the night. I was never that scared living in the middle of the madness of New York City. But the dead quiet of our bucolic backwoods, sliced with the screams of nature, twisted my imagination to the edge of reality. I barely slept and almost suffocated that night.

The following day, I learned from our lovely neighbors Lenore and Felix that the wild sounds I heard were just a pack of coyotes, which is common to the area. They laughed when I told them my reaction. I laugh about it myself now, too.

After twenty years of living in an Arcadian area like the Hudson Valley, I've learned to love the orchestral soundscape of creatures big and small that live in harmony around us. I actually get a charge out of listening to the conversations of community critters and wonder what they're saying. And I've developed a deep appreciation for nature and Mother Earth like never before. I became a gardener, a bird watcher, and a bug rescuer, and I'm more contemplative and reflective. I developed a closer relationship with the flowers, fauna, and all the living, breathing life surrounding us, keeping us alive. Moreover, I have a deepened sense of myself connected to nature as my home - our home. And it's in our home in the country that I found new dreams and inspiration. And decided to pursue something new.

Country Roads and Ramblings

"Adaptability is not imitation. It means power of resistance and assimilation" – Mahatma Gandhi

Adjusting to living in the country wasn't easy for quite some time. I had no friends, no job, and wasn't sure what I was going to do with myself in this new environment. And the fact that you have to drive everywhere was a reality that I begrudgingly had to accept. For all I knew, we could have moved to the countryside of England or somewhere on the outskirts of Alabama. I felt like a stranger in a strange land again, and much at a loss for leaving the familiarity and vibrancy of the city. I doubted that I could ever have much of a life again.

My first solo CD was released in February that year, 2004, when we moved upstate, which you would think would have been something to celebrate. I did quietly bask in the glory to a certain extent. I was thrilled about the accomplishment and satisfied with the music, the recording, working with great musicians, and all that went into the process. But unfortunately, the label didn't have the money for tour support, or much marketing to help attain the recognition and sales I had hoped for. The record did notably well, reaching number 35 on the Billboard Adult Contemporary Jazz Chart. Certainly a feather in my cap. But it still wasn't what I aspired to. Sadly, not long after, the label A440 Records went belly up.

"The rise and fall of A440 Music Group was, in many ways, a matter of timing. The 99-cent download had just launched, the iPod was just hitting the market, and streaming hadn't yet arrived, meaning music, for a time, was essentially free. Still, we took pride in every release: the design, the fidelity, the packaging. Machan's record was no exception. It was a beautiful album - musically rich, visually stunning - and a testament to her artistry." - Kent Anderson, former President, A440 Music Group

What the whole experience of making that record did do for me, however, was motivate me to get my guitar chops together and start playing gigs around the local area. At this point, I was into my forties, and I just didn't have the steam to venture out in a van and schlep around the country with my CDs in a trunk. Nevertheless, one thing led to another, and soon, I, a bass player Charlie Kniceley who was a longtime friend of Danny's, and drummer T.Xiques, were working three and four nights a week all over the local area and the New York Tri-state vicinity. Life had gone full circle.

For about four years, Charlie, T, and I hauled ourselves around to every restaurant, small concert venue, bar, private party, and even farmers' markets, peddling our wares to anyone who would listen. Once in a while, we even added additional players: a sax player, another guitar player, and a keyboard player to broaden the musical possibilities. But the core band was our little trio. We had a magnificent run, played a lot of music together, and immensely enjoyed each other's company. We made new friends and fans everywhere we played and made a lot of people happy. Moreover, it returned me to the reason I got into music as a teenager to begin with. Joy!

I realized that my years of being involved with high-profile tours and high-strung celebrity musicians, high on themselves and their status, somewhat damaged the pure pleasure of singing and playing music for me. It became a job. The job became more about navigating the politics, the drudgery of the lifestyle, and earning a living. The music only happened in the space in between everything else.

That, unfortunately, is what happens if you want a career as a working musician and artist in the music business. Don't get me wrong - it can be a wonderful business, depending on your level of success, involvement, and who you are as a person. But it is a business, not just a vocation, should you decide to make it your career. And if anyone expects to make a living in the business, it has to really be your business. There is no separating it out or half assed way to do it.

One can choose to play music for the sheer joy of it, be a weekend warrior doing occasional gigs, or record for oneself, and that's fine and lovely. But if you want more than that, there comes the tipping point where you fall into the world of it becoming your career pursuit. The glamorized ideal of being an artist, I believe, has been overblown by the American pop star-obsessed culture. It's become a perverted fantasy of fame and riches that's far from the real essence of what it means to be an artist. And it's a reality that will never materialize for most people who chase that hollow dream.

As I tell my students, you need to think about the truth of what you're going to do to make money to support your career aspirations once you graduate from college. Becoming an overnight million-dollar success is a rare phenomenon. And even then, it's difficult to sustain momentum enough in a music career to ensure it pays for your survival long-term, especially with the business model of the industry today. Therefore, it's essential to consider how you will financially support yourself, as well as nurture your creative pursuits.

If you want it badly enough, you'll figure out. Where there's a will there's a way. And surely, there are those who get lucky. I'm not saying that no one can "make it." There are artists breaking through it all the time. But the market is also gravely oversaturated, and the business model with streaming services and record companies controlling the revenue stream is not set up to support artists being able to sustain themselves. So don't count on becoming a YouTube sensation that goes viral and makes you a millionaire overnight. You need a realistic plan and a lot of ambition.

During that stretch of years of gigs playing with Charlie and T, I managed to score another record deal with another small record label called NuGroove Records, out of New Jersey. Motion of Love was released in 2007. While I thought it would be a second chance at solo career success, the experience was a repeat spin cycle. The label couldn't afford tour support, or the kind of marketing that would buttress building substantial achievement. So soon after, that label slowly faded into the shadows. And I was left holding a bag of beautifully produced songs, and the record label owning my masters. Fortunately, I was able to retrieve ownership of them not long ago.

The other important piece of this music business story is that the business itself was rapidly changing around the early 2000s. Many record label executives didn't understand how digital streaming and the internet would transform everything about the way the overall business would operate. They grossly underestimated how the digital domain would dominate how people would consume music and everything else. The concept of Napster, when it launched in 1999, was the canary in the coal mine. But many industry folks thought it was just a phase, like 8-track tape. They were perniciously wrong.

Anyhow, after another failed record deal, I was feeling despondent about what to do with my so-called music life. My restless spirit was getting the itch for another adventure, seeking to effectuate some unfulfilled desires for my personal growth, and get out of the rut that I was starting to feel with playing restaurants and bars. I had grown weary of people only listening in between bites of food, and as background to their conversations. I was finished feeling like wallpaper.

Ch, Ch, Ch, Changes

"Turn and face the strange..." - David Bowie

In 2011, at the age of 55, I chased a wild-haired idea and registered to take some college courses. I had been teaching voice privately for more than a decade in my home, in a few music stores, as well as at a private elementary school. However, I knew that I couldn't progress beyond that point without a college degree, if I wanted to enter the world of academia.

Empire State College, a division of the State University of New York, offered a unique program that allows students to earn credits toward a degree based on their life experience. It required a tremendous amount of work writing papers that explained and supported my knowledge base as it applied to my chosen degree program. Those papers collectively constructed a portfolio that was evaluated by a board of professors. They, in turn, awarded me my diploma.

Much of my undergraduate work was online or self-study for classes I was required to take, such as general education requirements. I had few in-person classes, which gave me freedom with my schedule, but also left me a bit detached and isolated. It took me a little over two years to complete my undergraduate program and get my bachelor's degree, which was amazing. At my age, time was of the essence. Everyone thought I was crazy!

Since I began working as a professional singer and musician in my teenage years, I skipped college and went directly into cultivating a career. I don't regret any part of that decision. I would never trade the prodigious life experiences I accumulated when I was young. I would have never had those experiences by going to college then. There simply isn't a substitute for experiential learning. No matter how many books you read, or Google searches you study, it's in the doing that you learn to become that thing you desire.

That said, I had always carried this sense that I missed out on the college experience. It also tied into my deep-rooted sense that I wasn't smart enough or good enough, which circles back to old ghosts. It's amazing how those early impressions permeate one's being-ness for life. Taking that step to attend college was my attempt to heal that ancient psychic fissure, and disprove the discordant ring of that tired chorus in my head.

After completing my Bachelor's degree in Music and Contemporary Voice, which was a no-brainer, I decided to go on to a master's degree. I was feeling so empowered about the accomplishment of my first degree that I wanted to prolong surfing that wave of confidence and keep soaking up more knowledge. I discovered how much I love learning, and wanted to savor that sensation. So I steamed ahead in search of a master's degree program.

I applied to the NYU Steinhardt Master's degree in Songwriting, which I thought would be relevant to my life and manageable, which it was. Amazingly, I was accepted to the program, even when applying after the deadline for applications. Thanks to the tremendous support and encouragement of Dr. Ron Sadoff, who was the chair of the department at the time, I started my master's degree program in September of 2014.

Pursuing my master's degree would turn out to be a completely different nut to crack than my undergrad program. I moved back into an apartment in NYC in order to go to school during the week and not have to commute two hours each way every day. That would've killed me. Through my dear friend Verna Gillis, I was able to connect with someone who had a great sublet apartment in the NYU buildings right near campus in Greenwich Village. I couldn't have gotten any closer to school, nor could I have asked for a better situation.

My classes were in person at NYU as opposed to online in the privacy of my home. There I was, at 58 years old now, sitting in classrooms with Gen Zers and feeling like an interloper, a transgenerational squatter, and an outsider once again. It was boorish and distressing. What was I doing? Was I out of my mind? Who am I to think I can do this? What do these kids think of me? The internal voices prattled around the reverb chamber of my self-doubt.

The crossfire cacophony of my internal critics was having a field day in my post-menopausal brain, which was already wrestling with the fated biological makeover I was experiencing. Wasn't that enough for me to deal with? Women of a certain age know exactly what I'm talking about. Why was I putting myself through this self-inflicted torment at this point in my life? It was one of the most mentally and emotionally demanding phases I can remember. And perhaps one of the most constructive periods in my character development. It's true what they say: What doesn't kill you makes you stronger.

I got myself back into therapy when I started my program at NYU. Along with that, I developed IBS, high blood pressure, and an autoimmune disease. Oh boy! Dis-ease... I was so ill at ease, which says it all. I felt like I was spinning in a centrifugal acceleration machine with maximum G-force, stuck to the imaginary walls of psychological dread.

I also observed, for the first time, the internal politics that occur between professors and university administration, and how that spills out onto students. I learned there are some very big egos in academia. Like any industry I suppose.

There was one teacher in particular who clearly didn't like me. He struck me as an arrogant charlatan who could get away with his B.S. with 18-year-olds. And he somehow sucked up to the administration in the just the right way to keep his position. But it was easy for me, as an adult, to see through his facade. And I think he knew it. He was a frustrated musician and a marginally successful songwriter who ended up teaching - I assume not by choice.

Sadly, there are many teachers out there who don't come to the profession with love and passion, but rather come begrudgingly out of necessity, and bitter that they didn't become rock stars in their fields. Or couldn't decide what to do with their lives while in college. Of course that's not true overall. There are incredible teachers out there who are inspirational angels, guiding young minds to reach their greatness. But I've witnessed a few that lack the luster and compassion to be doing that work.

Meanwhile, simultaneously with my study program, I was fortunate enough to secure a part-time teaching position at the Clive Davis Institute of Recorded Music at Tisch-NYU, as a voice teacher. So I was juggling wearing different personality hats, different power positions, and a boatload of work that even someone in their twenties would have found head spinning. But somehow, I survived. In hindsight, it may have been an extraneous amount to take on. But I learned so much, had a great experience, earned my degree, and nurtured the teaching skills that I continue to practice and treasure to this day. And remember those maternal instincts I had locked away? They found the perfect place to live in my teaching role with my students. So in a sense, I finally have some kids. Lots of them in fact. It's wonderful!

Going back to school taught me an appreciation of the value of higher education: further developing my intellect, learning better critical thinking, exploring the processes of my own mind, and building character. Depending on the subject and material you're studying, higher education expands your consciousness and sense of self in relation to the world around you. It should be an essential part of an individual's development. I believe it should be required and provided for everyone, everywhere - at least an undergraduate degree. I believe we would be living in a more intelligent and evolved society, especially here in America at this time.

That, and travel - everyone should be required to go to far and distant places around the world. Exposure to and connection with other people, cultures, and ways of living can help one move away from cultural egocentrism and nationalism. It shapes a more expansive and inclusive understanding of the world. Maybe not for all, but for most. It diverts you out of your comfort zone and surmounts small-mindedness. Geographically and spiritually, it can be wonderfully expansive and humbling all at once.

"Travel is fatal to prejudice, bigotry, and narrow-mindedness, and many of our people need it sorely on these accounts. Broad, wholesome, charitable views of men and things cannot be acquired by vegetating in one little corner of the earth all one's lifetime." - Mark Twain, The Innocents Abroad / Roughing It

    I'm grateful for the many opportunities I had to travel extensively throughout my years on tour. Travel gave me a breadth of acceptance and compassion for other human beings and their ways of living. It opened my eyes and ears to different languages and ways of communicating. Perhaps the most enjoyable part of those experiences was that they deliciously awakened my palate to the myriad of fantastic flavors that exist in the world. This deepened my appreciation and compassion for my fellow citizens on the planet. Food and the enjoyment of it are a fundamental, unifying human pleasure. It's a powerful vehicle of communion in such a delightful way.
    Those broadening adventures in my life taught me that we truly are all essentially the same as human beings. We all want to be respected and loved. We all want to feel a sense of purpose and meaning in our lives. We all desire to enjoy creature comforts with family and friends. We all want a sense of safety, no matter where we live. And we all want to be happy. What else is there, really? None of that understanding came from a book.
    Beyond that, money, fame, and accolades are just egotistical constructs that we humans have convinced ourselves are of crucial importance. In the end, none of that will matter. What will matter is how we lived and loved and the memories we've taken and left behind.

"In the end, the love you take is equal to the love you make" - Paul McCartney

Time Waits for No One

"Your absence has gone through me like thread through a needle. Everything I do is stitched with its color" - W.S. Merwin

On April 17th, 2012, my heart was cracked to its core when my little dog Luna died. A five-pound fur ball, a pitbull trapped in a Maltese body, had been my main companion for what seemed a lifetime. He was with me during the dissolution of my first marriage. He accompanied me through the loss of my other dog, his older sister Suki. He was with me when I first moved back to NYC, before I met Danny. We entered that relationship with Danny together, where we all became a family. He helped me manage the transition from the concrete jungle to softer, greener pastures. He was my cuddle companion through countless nights of being alone while Danny was on the road. And he was a consistent part of the pleasure of my daily routine for sixteen years. Those of you who own and love dogs know that it's a responsibility that becomes a big focus of your life. It's one of the greatest, sweetest, and most unconditional forms of love a human can have with a non-human companion. Dogs are the best.

I loved that crazy canine more than anything else in my life. I had always had dogs as a child, but I couldn't keep them for much of my adult life because of my gypsy lifestyle. When I came back to NYC with Suki and then got Luna, he was a significant, stable force that helped me to feel grounded. I completely understand the trend for people to have therapy pets these days. Animals are all about love in ways that even the most incredible humans can't be.

By the time Luna was about sixteen years old, he was basically blind, deaf, and somewhat incontinent. He was getting to the end of his doggie time for a little dog. But he had had a really good life. He had a better life than many humans have. But it was a privilege for me to provide him with the best of everything I could.

When he finally passed, it was as if I had lost a limb. I felt the pain of his loss so deeply. It was much worse than my divorce from my first husband, or losing the gig with Sting. Perhaps because I didn't have children, my maternal feelings were projected onto him. Surely, it's some of what I transfer over to my students now.

As I started to recover from the devastation of losing him, it was right about the time that I was thinking about going on to a master's degree. In hindsight, Luna's passing when he did freed me up to take on the significant transition of returning to NYC and school. I sometimes think that he planned it that way; letting me go so I could move on with my life. In a strange way, he did me a favor.

A few years after that agonizing event, my mother passed. Following several years of rough going with her mental and physical health, she moved, at the age of ninety-one, out of our family home in New Jersey. She moved in with my older sister for a short time, which I think was the beginning of the end for her. My mother had never remarried after my father died in 1986, so she was used to being alone. Too much so. But the loss of her independence, the ability to drive, and the only home in America she knew spun her into a more profound depression than she was already in. She attempted suicide at my sister's house, and ended up in a psychiatric ward for a month.

After that distressing episode, my mother landed with my younger brother, his wife, and young daughter. I thought for a minute that that arrangement might be good for her, with young energy around. But her days deteriorated into sitting in her bedroom, with all her possessions, watching TV while quietly mumbling to herself about how she didn't want to be alive. It was tragic to watch my mother give up on life. Her mind and her heart were withered, like my garden starved of water for a week. But somehow the vehicle of her body was ticking away and keeping her alive.

Truthfully, I know my mother was clinically depressed for most of her adult life after coming to America. She would have benefited greatly from some therapy and perhaps medication at some point. It may have transformed the outcome of her life. But her Japanese pride and fear wouldn't allow it. She had to keep up her face, like many of her generation and culture. So left unchecked at her advanced age, the darkness pulled her down to an unreachable depth. It was heartbreaking to witness. It relegated those of us around her to a helpless, emotional void.

After about a year of my mother living with my brother, she contracted pneumonia. She ended up deathly ill in the hospital for several weeks. We all thought it was the end. But somehow, she beat the virus, however weakened and frail. Not only had she been worn down by the illness, but she was also diagnosed with peripheral artery disease. Basically, her body was literally shutting down. And most likely it had been for some time.

We transferred Mom to a nursing home that was located halfway between my brother's house in Pennsylvania and mine in upstate New York. Since it was the summer, I was off from school, affording me the time to visit her regularly. The drive was an hour and a half each way for both my brother and me, which, sadly, he was displeased about.

After several weeks in the nursing home, I thought my mother's condition might be stabilizing. So I decided to decorate and cozy up her room for what I thought would be an extended stay. I brought her favorite green floral quilt, some family photos, and familiar knick-knacks, warming up the antiseptic decorum of the institutional setting.

That day I decorated, we had a lovely, long visit. I gave her a manicure and pedicure. We talked. I brought her some Japanese sweets that she seemed to enjoy. I got her out of her room and wheeled her around the nursing home lounge to say hello to some fellow residents. It was a good day overall. When it finally came time to say good night, I gave her a kiss and told her I loved her, promising that I'd return in just a few days. It was a sweet departure. But lying beneath the niceties was a din of dread with leaving her.

Early the next morning, the nursing home called to say that my mother had passed quietly during the night. The peripheral arterial disease had finally calcified her vessels so much that it had stopped her heart. I take solace in the thought that she died peacefully in her sleep. She deserved a peaceful passing after enduring such a difficult life.

There is nothing like losing your mother, regardless of what kind of relationship you've had. A mother symbolizes the very portal of flesh and bone that birthed you into the world. She is the root of your identity. And we're forever connected via the mystical umbilical cord. There is no other love or relationship that is as intimate and profound. It's unexplainable. The minute I heard my mother had passed, I felt like an orphan.

I've learned, as we all must learn, that loss is a part of life. I strive to live with the acceptance of that fact and with the guidance of the Buddhist Noble Truths. Dukkha: The Truth of Suffering: Pain is inevitable, but suffering is not; is fairly simple to grasp. We always have a choice in how we deal with loss and pain. We can choose to be angry or feel victimized. Or gracefully accept the bitterness along with the sweetness of existence. No one escapes the cycle of life and death, joy and sorrow, yin and yang. But we can control how we endure the experience.

The other Noble Truths are more challenging for me, which is why they call it a practice, I suppose. Letting go of attachment (Samudaya) to desires and cravings is hard in this materialistic world. I'm still a bit of a hungry ghost, wanting to soak up all the hedonistic pleasure I can while existing in the flesh, awake in this carton of consciousness, frolicking through this physical stratum. For that, no doubt I'll be back a few more times.

Nirodha, the cessation of suffering, I'll have to work on along with the previous two truths. And Magga, the Eight Fold Path to the cessation of suffering, is a process I'm working on slowly in baby steps. It's a practical method to achieve liberation, through the practice of Right Understanding, Right Thought, Right Speech, Right Action, Right Livelihood, Right Effort, Right Mindfulness, and Right Concentration. All such good goals for a well-lived, enlightened life. But like I said, this isn't my last rodeo.

While I believe in reincarnation, I don't know of anyone who's definitively proven their return from a previous life form. I know that there are those who claim to remember their past lives. And I myself have had numerous deja vu experiences. But who's to say?

On the other hand, I also believe in science and the basic principle in physics that energy can never be destroyed, only transformed. So wouldn't it make sense that the essence of who we are never dies? And perhaps that essence is the soul, that this life energy that has always existed, always will? And that the energy we call the life force just keeps evolving and transforming infinitely? It sounds like the closest definition of God to me. And that, by the way, is dog backwards.

Luna

A nice moment with mom later in her life

Going Forward

"It's hard to know how to go forward, if you don't know where you've been" - Jane Fonda

It's strange to contemplate one's own mortality. It's a privilege you're awarded only if you live long enough. Or perhaps if you encounter some life-threatening disease, an accident, or a traumatic event that stops you in your tracks, and in turn forces a serious review of your existence.

It was just yesterday that I could eat and drink anything and not gain weight. I could stay up all night and party with no thought about the consequences to my body. I pretty much looked the same for a long time. Time felt like it would tick on forever. I felt invincible. It's the blessing and the curse of youth.

Today, my reflection in the mirror has certainly changed. My internal chemistry has regenerated and renewed many decades over. My life experiences have left me with more behind than ahead. I can sense the mark of time on my being and body. I savor the storylines etched into the pathway of my heart. Perhaps more importantly, I acknowledge character traits that no longer define me or serve me, belonging to the earlier versions of myself. Change is good. But it's not always easy to adopt the new and let go of the old.

During my recent psychedelic therapy sessions, I experienced clear visions of the continuum of the life energy that I'm a part of; that we're all a part of. I felt the seamless ebb and flow that intertwines past, present, and future into a single, unending tapestry. I traveled along the river of ever-moving timeless essence, which carries us all silently along its embracing currents. In those moments of deep reflection, I could feel myself as a tiny, shimmering drop within this grand stream of life, connected to countless other drops that came before, are present, and will come after me.

There was a profound serenity in recognizing that we are both fleeting and eternal - brief moments of consciousness embedded within a boundless eternity. That sense of being a part of this grand, bigger-than-life force, is humbling and awe-inspiring.

In those extraordinary states of consciousness and moments of realization, I can deeply appreciate the miracle that I have manifested into this physical plane at this time, surrounded by an invisible flow of the inexplicable. I could sense my grandmother and other ancestors there next to me, embracing me with their love and support, letting me know that I am ok, and destined someday to join them in the continuum. It's life. It's samsara. It's the cosmic rhythm of the universe. The eternal dance we are all dancing.

In the psychedelic world and the religious world, you would say I've had a mystical experience. Perhaps some of you are thinking that you don't need either drugs or dogma to find that intersection of life and the divine. And I would agree. I've had many mystical experiences completely sober through beautiful music, meditation, communing with nature, great works of art, or special moments with people. But there is a compounded depth I've encountered via the psychedelic route that's beyond words. I know the powerful propulsion of those experiences metamorphosed my being, all for the better, in an instant.

Time, and those transformative experiences, have helped to bring me to this present place of greater peace. I've arrived at this moment in life with the resolve that every season, every chapter, every person, and every thing I've encountered needed to happen in order for me to evolve into the person I am now. And furthermore, who I will evolve into tomorrow, again and again. So as I see it now, there's no good, bad, or indifferent to my experiences of the past. It's all just been an essential part of the grand design of this life journey, every puzzle piece fitting together to create the whole picture. The caterpillar to the cocoon.

Everything needed to happen, the way it happened, for the flowering of the butterfly's dream.

I may still be in the chrysalis phase of my development, but I can sense my wings forming and new horizons emerging. The very process of writing this book has been alchemic, a transmutation into a richer version of myself. Cathartic. An unearthing of the gold that's been waiting to be mined.

Though it's a time of great uncertainty and unrest in America, I still look to the future with hope and optimism as my foundation. I look forward to these last chapters of my life with enthusiasm, eager to continue growing, meet new challenges, and embrace the process of aging with grace. It's a blessing to still be here.

All the internal work I've done, and the review of my life, has brought me to a more authentic sense of myself. It's given me a knowingness that only comes with ego death to the process. To uncover one's willingness to investigate behind the shield of one's persona, in order to eventually find one's true self. I've discovered the deviant pleasure of diving into the interior of my own psychic abyss, no matter how uncomfortable or painful. And I discovered the appreciation for this long, twisted sojourn, no matter how unfinished it continues to feel.

The older I get, the more I realize that life is like the Golden Spiral. It's about living in a way to find the beauty and balance that are meant to be. It's the search for spiritual homeostasis. And it's what is embedded in our code of existence. That code exists in all of us and all of nature around us. It's the Fibonacci sequence. It's Sacred Geometry. It bridges the gap between the tangible and the mystical.

There, amid whatever chaos that exists on the surface of our world, there is a beautifully harmonious state that lies within, waiting to be discovered. Underneath the turbulence and madness, a self-correcting mechanism is figuring out how to manifest. There in the heart of the Golden Spiral is the testament of the interconnectedness of everything in the cosmos. And beneath the fears and illusions lies a magnetic core of truth and balance, which in the end will attract all things into its orbit. Ultimately, I believe that love will prevail.

However, in order to reach the maxim of existence, we must be willing to voyage through the tribulations of the spiral path. We're so far away from that now as a species. It requires that we learn to speak the language of the soul. We must learn to honor the rhythms of nature, respect the earth, and bow to the universe, as all native and indigenous people once did. It's there where we can find the secrets to life itself and uncover the magic of existence that we've forgotten. It's there, I believe, where we can truly make sense of it all.

Ramble On... Sing My Song

"Life is like riding a bicycle. To keep your balance, you must keep moving" - Albert Einstein

It's been over twenty-five years now that teaching has been a primary focus in my work life. I've spent over ten years at the Clive Davis Institute at NYU. Simultaneously, for six years, I taught at the New School of Jazz and Contemporary Music, instructing in voice, songwriting, and performance - a position I've recently decided to relinquish to make more room for myself and my own projects. Never in my youth did I imagine this to be the picture of my life. Yet, as I reached back into my family's history, I realized that I had unconsciously followed in the footsteps of several ancestors who were teachers.

My heart overflows with joy and fulfillment at what the teaching profession has given me. To be of service, to pay forward my knowledge and experience, to share love and support with aspiring young artists, and to stay vibrant and relevant - it's rewarded me with an immense sense of accomplishment that surpasses anything I could have imagined.

In this chapter of life, I've found a sense of authenticity, self-realization, and truth. Not that my life as a professional singer and all that work I did prior wasn't honest or didn't fulfill me. It has been an incredible ride, and it's not over. My music career memories are jewels woven into the fabric of my identity. I treasure it all. But now, it's no longer the predominant motif of my life's purpose. Time has transmuted the landscape as it should. It has carved the flow of the river of my life through new wondrous territories. The past has become the vital architecture I stand on. And the foundation from where I can rearrange the music as I wish, like moving furniture around my house. I see my life now from a higher vantage point and from a position of strength. Like a Catbird, I'm in a really good place.

I don't harbor regret or clutch onto anger towards my parents or events of my past anymore. It's a kite lost to the wind. Nor do I feel victim to how my life panned out. Though it has taken me some time to tease out what emotional baggage belongs to me and what belongs to others, I know I no longer need to carry useless dead weight. It's taken time to comb through the jungle of ganglion emotional threads and crawl through tunnels of emotional sewage to arrive at the clearing field.

I'm so grateful that my parents gave me this life. I know they did the best they could with what little they had. My siblings, though estranged, are the family I was assigned to on this earth's mission, although I've yet to fully understand why. But I can finally let go of the guilt I dragged around for years, that I somehow betrayed them by making something of myself. They are who they are, and they need to solve their own mysteries. I don't need to fix them, or anyone for that matter. It's just unfortunate that we operate on entirely different wavelengths and speak a different language of the heart. But I love them and accept what is. Additionally, I now understand how all my past romantic and professional relationships were valuable stepping stones and teaching moments, rather than failures. And how I continue to grow supported by the bedrock of those experiences.

Everything happens for a reason. I've witnessed the evidence of that for myself. From my first marriage to my career, there are a million ways things could have unfolded for me. When I look back, it's astounding how I've had this colorful kaleidoscope of experiences, enough for a few lifetimes over. How fortunate I've been.

I liken my unfolding to the theory of observation in quantum physics. Observing something changes the nature and behavior of the thing you're observing. Particles can exist in multiple states simultaneously. So, then, can our realities manifest and play out in various ways. And much of that manifestation is our choice. Consciously or not.

As Socrates posited, "The unexamined life is not worth living." Cheers to that. Beyond that, with the knowledge of the self, we acquire the magnificent power to change.

"You take the blue pill, the story ends, you wake up in your bed and believe whatever you want to believe. You take the red pill, you stay in Wonderland, and I show you how deep the rabbit hole goes." - The Matrix

Whether it be a metaphysical, psychological, or spiritual perspective, we can choose how our lives unfold. We can rewrite our stories and change the narratives and trajectories. I know because I've done it. That said, it takes courage to take the road less traveled. It's hard to swallow that red pill. And there's no turning back.

The big lesson I've learned is that the deeper the well of pain in one's life, along with the willingness to go into and through the fire, the greater the reward of joy and love there is to be discovered. I'm not claiming that I've figured it all out. Or that I no longer have work to do. That's far from the truth. Growth is a lifelong process. Possibly longer. But I'm in for the long haul.

Can you imagine if our educational systems prioritized teaching everyone how to nurture good mental and emotional health, just as math, science, and art are taught? Can you imagine if people around the world, including political leaders, were required to honestly reflect upon their own internal worlds, and held accountable to do the work to heal themselves? It would be a very different kind of world.

For now, I embrace being an insatiable seeker, the composer of this cacophonous concerto of me. And I'll continue to search for those singing a similar song. Till my dying days, I'll be reaching for everything I can to enrich my being with more beauty and truth. I'll continue to gather more realizations and clarity about what it means to be alive and human. And hopefully, as I journey through whatever time I have left, I'll keep singing my song to whomever will listen, while I scatter speckles of my existence like stardust, to evince to the universe that I am and was here.

As Einstein said, keep pedaling and moving forward.

Rock on!

Acknowledgements

"We cannot live only for ourselves. A thousand fibers connect us with our fellow men"- Herman Melville

To the dynamic Eileen Shapiro for generously connecting me with Teddie Dahlin and New Haven Publishing. I can't thank you all enough for taking a chance on me and helping me birth this baby. Thanks to Margaret Daisley, who read the first draft of my manuscript and provided invaluable feedback and cheered me on. To my sister-in-law, Laura Stokes, who likely suffered through reading my story, but was kind enough to share her thoughts lovingly. Thank you Sarah Healey for your editing energy and patience with my file management.

Marcene and Danny O'Bryen, your friendship for over forty years has been as consistent and true as the sunrise. Love you madly. Dougal Caron, I love that you're still in my life. Grover Kemble, Dave Miller, Tim Solook, and John Gatti, you're my first musical family. Jed DeFilippis, calling me for the Jackson Victory Tour changed the trajectory of my life. May you rest in blissful peace. Elisabeth Oei, time and space have widened between us, but you have a special place in my heart. Emily Horowitz - You know, thank you! To all the musicians and singers I've worked with over the years, I'm so lucky to have shared so many stages and to have made so much great music with you all. Special smooches to Elaine Caswell and Sophia Ramos. To my Gov't Mule family and Pink Floyd fans everywhere, thank you for years of beautiful messages and support. Shout out to my Upstate New York tribe: Bruce, Verna, Donna, Harvey, Julie, Chris, Barbara, David, Charlie, Susan, Mike, Pam, and my extended hang gang. To Celina, Victor and Bruce, you're my sweet Danish honey buns. Amy Schliftman, rocks! Big thanks to Nick Sansano at the Clive Davis Institute of Recorded Music/NYU for opening the door to my treasured teaching life. Brianne Hayes you're the amazing mama bear that keeps it all going. To my colleagues with whom I'm so proud to be in the same league. To all my students, past, present, and future: you're my big, beautiful, blessing. Extending an olive branch to my siblings Miki, Jacqueline, John and their families. The waters have thinned the viscosity of our bond, but I'm still here for you if you want.

Last but definitely not least, my amazingly multi-talented, intelligent, smart-assed husband Danny, who has had my back through thick and thin, creative projects, school, and life's unpredictable twists. You are my loyal lion, my boxing partner, my miracle. We're in this together, whether you like it or not.

About the Author

Machan Taylor is a lifelong artist whose four-decade career has taken her from world tours and major recordings to creative mentorship and teaching. A singer, songwriter, and performer, she has shared the stage with artists including Sting, Pink Floyd, Pat Benatar, George Benson, Gov't Mule and more, and was the lead vocalist for the Grammy-nominated group Hiroshima. Her solo album *Machan* debuted #35 on the Billboard Contemporary Jazz Charts, and her compositions have appeared on television and in award-winning films.

Equally at home in the classroom as on the stage, Machan is a NCVS Certified Vocologist and sought-after voice teacher who helps singers develop healthy and authentic artistry. She holds a Master's Degree in Music Theory and Composition from New York University. She served as Vocal Coach and Associate Producer for Vera Farmiga's film *Higher Ground* and is currently an Adjunct Professor at NYU's Clive Davis Institute of Recorded Music. She continues to create, teach, and inspire as a performer and now as an author. She hopes to have another dog someday.

www.ingramcontent.com/pod-product-compliance
Lightning Source LLC
Chambersburg PA
CBHW050926240426
43670CB00022B/2947